CERTAIN THINGS ABOUT MY MOTHER

ABOUT MY MOTHER

DAUGHTERS SPEAK

Edited by **Susan Musgrave**

ANNICK PRESS

TORONTO + NEW YORK + VANCOUVER

© 2003 Introduction, Susan Musgrave; "Certain Things About My Mother," Melanie Little; "If You Can't Be Good," Nancy Lee; "Wherever You Are," Priscila Uppal; "In the Silence that Speaks," Sue Goyette; "So Much," Hiromi Goto; "The Sound of Dishes in the Sink," Taien Ng-Chan; "What You Don't Know," Gayla Reid

Annick Press Ltd.

We acknowledge the support of the Canada Council for the Arts, the Ontario Arts Council, and the Government of Canada through the Book Publishing Industry Development Program (BPIDP) for our publishing activities.

Edited by Barbara Pulling
Copy-edited by Pam Robertson
Cover and interior design by Irvin Cheung/iCheung Design
Cover models: Mozhgan Navidi and Niloofar Akhavan (a real-life mother and daughter)
Cover photograph by Storme
Fashion Stylist: Amy Lu

Cataloguing in Publication Data

    Certain things about my mother : daughters speak / edited by Susan Musgrave.

    ISBN 1-55037-812-0 (pbk.)   ISBN 1-55037-813-9 (bound)

    1. Mothers and daughters. 2. Teenage girls. 3. Parent and teenager.
4. Women authors, Canadian (English)—20th century—Biography.
I. Musgrave, Susan, 1951-

HQ755.85.C43 2003   306.874'3   C2003-900803-7

The text was typeset in Bembo.

Printed and bound in Canada

Distributed in Canada by	**Distributed in the U.S.A. by**	**Published in the U.S.A. by**
Firefly Books Ltd.	Firefly Books (U.S.) Inc.	Annick Press (U.S.) Ltd.
3680 Victoria Park Avenue	P.O. Box 1338	
Willowdale, ON	Ellicott Station	
M2H 3K1	Buffalo, NY 14205	

visit us at **www.annickpress.com**

CONTENTS

INTRODUCTION

MY MOTHER COULD HAVE BEEN MY OLDER SISTER when I was a teenager. She was ageless, it seemed to me. Vivacious. Witty. Flirtatious, in an innocent sort of way. "He that would the daughter win / Must with the mother first begin," goes a seventeenth-century proverb. In our twentieth-century household there was no competition: any boyfriend I managed to lure home laid eyes on my mother and fell in love.

They adored her baking, too: the cake and cookie tins in our house were always filled, and she never "cheated" by using a mix. She also made her own bread, but her home-made strawberry jam would soak through my sandwiches by lunchtime, and I envied the other kids their normal Wonder Bread—*their* sandwiches didn't look like gauze bandages with crusts. My mother was thrifty to a fault, washing the wax paper she wrapped my sandwiches in, setting it to dry over the transistor radio, and reusing it until I surreptitiously threw it out. She plastered flower-power decals all over her car, read books, and had even written poetry herself and had it published when she was at school. My friends thought she was cool. I wanted her to be normal, the way I thought my friends' mothers were. "I'll never end up like her," I promised myself.

My mother had dreams for me, including the one where she didn't want me learning about sex in the back seat of a car. "Then why don't you leave me at home when the rest of you go out on the boat every weekend?" I'd argue. "That way I can learn about sex in my own bed." That's how I remember it, but I doubt that either of us would have actually used the word "sex" at the time.

In each of the seven essays in this collection, I found parts of both my mother and myself. "Sex was never mentioned in our home," Nancy Lee says in "If You Can't Be Good." "I may not be lovable, but my mother loves me," Hiromi Goto writes of herself as a teen. "When my nerves aren't jangling from a fight with my mother, I'm often walking around in a haze of bafflement," says Melanie Little, "trying to figure out how human beings can sustain such nastiness." "I have feelings too!" Tien Ng-Chan's mother shouts, when she's finally had enough; her daughter screams "I HATE YOU!" and slams the front door.

Gayla Reid, in "What You Don't Know," can tell her mother everything — or just about. Sue Goyette's mother takes a job and leaves her daughter in the role of surrogate mother, cooking the meals and protecting her siblings from a frustrated, difficult father. I may have felt betrayed by my mother (she sided with my father, so that I was forced to spend my weekends anchored in lonely coves rather than at home experimenting with drugs and sex), but I was never motherless the way Priscila Uppal had been left. In "Wherever You Are," the story of her mother's unexplained disappearance, she tells of the effects abandonment has had on a daughter who could earn everything—scholarships, degrees, a best-seller, marriage, children of her own—except a mother's love.

The seven women who rose to the challenge of writing—truthfully and often painfully—about their relationships with their mothers are to be commended for their courage. I've heard it said that the last thing any parent wants is for their child to become a writer. Writers are well-known pillagers of privacy; sooner or later we zoom in on our own pain, and unhappy family secrets can get exposed in the process. What we write may upset those close to us, and if we go on to publish our work, they may feel deeply betrayed. I suspect my own mother asks herself, every time I bring out a new book, "Where did I go wrong?"

This insightful collection of personal stories is destined to go out into the world and live a brave, new life of its own. The words written here will make you laugh and cry, and I hope you'll find them a comfort as you struggle with your own mother to become the woman you want to be. I hope, too, that the mothers of these seven extraordinary writers will be proud enough to say to themselves, after reading this book, not "Where did I go wrong?" but "I seem to have done something right."

—Susan Musgrave

CERTAIN THINGS ABOUT MY MOTHER

MELANIE LITTLE

"My Dear Mother," I write. "I am composing this letter not in the heat of the moment or on a passing whim but after long and careful thought. This is a serious letter. Please . . . I beg you . . . take it in the same spirit of urgency with which it was written."

My mother and I have had another of our fights. One of the tsunami ones, the kind that come out of nowhere, or maybe out of an unseen tremor deep in the belly of the earth. They grow and grow, these things, until they are monstrous, unstoppable, able to wipe out entire towns. And then they retreat, a wash of suddenly placid water, as if they'd never been. My mother will usually come into my room an hour or so after they're over to kiss me good-night, her whisper the lap of a soft wave against unyielding rock. (Unyielding, though I always lie awake, waiting, until she comes in.)

The letter is my way of saying I've had enough of our destructive little dance. (Also, as can probably be detected from its talcum-powdery tone, I've been reading a lot of two-hundred-year-old epistolary novels lately.) "The situation has become intolerable," my missive continues. "One moment, everything is rosy, and we are the best of friends; the next, you turn on me, and I feel like I can't do anything right. All I want to do is flee, but you won't stop attacking until you've exhausted us both, and then the next day it's like nothing ever happened . . . until it starts again. I'm at my limit, and I'm sure, Mom, that you are too. I think from now on it would be wisest if we avoided talking to each other whenever possible. I'm leaving for university in less than a year; I think we can survive until then by treating each other with cordiality and common courtesy but not venturing into any actual conversations, since those always seem to get us into such infernal waters. Please know that I only want to do this because I think it's best for us in the long run. I love you and respect you more than anything else in the world, and I want to keep both of those feelings unspoiled." In case I haven't made myself clear, I end by re-sounding the keynote: "Things can*not* continue between us as they are!"

I don't end up giving my mother this letter, though for about a week I leave it in my night-table drawer so she'll find it if she tries to snoop in my diary, a deed I've suspected her of in the past. I plant a white thread on top of it as a marker, certain to fall unnoticed—by her—if she picks the letter up. After a week of it remaining untouched, I hide the letter away somewhere less inviting.

But I do haul it out from time to time—when I want to marvel at the wisdom and maturity of my words, for example, or when I feel like a good, self-righteous cry.

The fights, the tsunamis, continue their endless cycle of come and go.

"You have a mean streak," I once heard my father shout at my mother, when he was on the receiving end of one of her rages. But if this is true, then I have to believe the streak is only a path, a conduit, for the furious energy running through her and then back out. Yes, she is an angry person. Maybe, probably. But overall, I'm pretty sure she's a good person, too, vulnerable as dried rose petals, far from mean.

Other people, though, *many* other people, do seem to have a hot, thick stripe of cruelty stretching from their eyes to their toes. When my nerves aren't jangling from a fight with my mother, I'm often walking around in a haze of bafflement, trying to figure out how human beings can sustain such nastiness. The truth is, I'm half-afraid of most of my "peers," the way I'm afraid of big, feisty dogs with powerful legs and jaws. And like dogs, the nasty ones can smell my fear. In general, I keep my distance. Yet still they cross my path.

Lately, I've developed a bedtime ritual, not all that different, really, from the way some people say their prayers or count sheep. I lie in bed, close my eyes, and carry out (silently, of course) the roll call of the day's prisoners. The girl who laughed sarcastically when I bungled a question in my least favorite class, physics. The kids in front of me this afternoon at the play our English teacher took us to, a whole row of bimbos and boneheads giggling and squirming around like their pants were full of bugs, talking loudly enough to make the thrown-off actors look our way. After school, the hipster in the silver BMW, hurtling around the corner so fast he'd have knocked me flat if I hadn't lurched out of his path in time. He didn't even look back at my one-finger salute, too busy jawing on his bite-sized cell phone.

I don't like violence. I don't want to hurt these people physically, not even in my imagination, no matter how heinous their crimes. I only want to teach them a lesson. Usually, this lesson involves locking them together in an elevator for the night. The elevator in question is only a little larger than a coffin, and it requires a key to make it operate — a key I keep fast in the pocket of my mind. It's the most fitting punishment I can think of, this tomblike imprisonment with a bunch of strangers every bit as obnoxious as themselves. For a few minutes each night, I lie in the dark and imagine what the worst people in my day might have to say to each other in such a circumstance, what each of them might miss most about their perfect, ordered, daylight existences. But I fall asleep quickly. With my victims locked away, the world is a safe place for me to dream and roam.

There are, of course, times when I'm angry enough with my mother to lock her in that elevator too. But she knows she doesn't belong there, and the combination of her shock and my guilt annihilate any pleasure the fantasy might have given me. "How could you do this to me?" she seems to say, and her hurt rises up and out of a tiny airhole in the elevator like a fine red mist, filling and filling my bedroom with its grievance.

Once my mother threw a ten-pound toy truck, steel, at my dad's head. Her mother, my grandma, was the same. When I was a kid, Grandma would watch calmly as I yanked down her curtains, tore out treasures from her drawers and cupboards, and turned her immaculate house upside down to construct pirate forts, supermarket displays, labyrinthine Batgirl caves. But when my grandpa came home and dripped tiny drops of mud onto the carpet, she'd chase him around in a froth, swinging a frying pan at his head.

My mom maintains that her own grandmother died of spontaneous combustion, that one morning she suddenly burst into flames and perished. I used to think this was a joke. But more and more, I figure Great-Grandma Major just got really mad at something. I can imagine the quick heating of her flesh, the burnt smell of her hair, a loud *pop*. I can believe, when it comes right down to it, anything about the women in my family.

The kids at school don't talk about their mothers much. Maybe the subject is uncool. Maybe they're like me, loaded up with fresh anecdotes every morning but swallowing them all down with massive effort, forever biting their tongues. It's true that when people's mothers *do* make a narrative appearance, it's usually to be mad about something. "My mo-om was sooo pissed," someone will say. Usually, the person is talking about getting caught at some outrageous exploit that would cause *my* mother to jump screaming off a cliff with me in tow, like necking with their pants off or stealing the answers to an exam or snorting crystal meth in the bathroom at school. Given these crimes, "sooo pissed" seems like the coolest, most enviable of understatements. Most parents would probably kill to have a goody-two-shoes kid like me — my mother even says so herself in her more pro-Melanie moods. I really believe this, I guess, that I am God's gift to parenthood, and that's what makes her rages so hard to take.

It's confusing. I have to admit that the few big things I've done have scarcely made my mother blink. I've failed tests, stolen and promptly ruined her best clothes, come home smelling like a distillery while insisting I've been at the library. I even quit figure skating after my parents had invested ten years of their lives and all of their money in it. And there was my mom, telling me she understood, she was young once, I am still the best daughter in the whole wide world. No, it's things like me leaving crumbs on the counter or asking, well in advance, if I can accept a rare and crucial invitation to go out to a movie on a school night: these are the things that have the power to light her spark and send her — both of us — up into the ether.

Maybe it's like Mr. Martin, our physics teacher, said. *The universe is fundamentally unknowable.* That's what he made us copy down on the first day of grade twelve. A couple of wiseasses got up as if to leave, arguing that if the universe was unknowable, there was no point in sitting through physics class. Although Mr. Martin is no personal favorite of mine, his words stuck with me.

Case in point: for two unbelievable (not as in "great"; as in "impossible to believe") weeks, I have a boyfriend.

Generally, if boys talk to me it's to ask if they can copy my homework. Jamie, the boyfriend-boy, is beautiful, too, and what's more, he's cool. I spend fourteen days on constant, terrified lookout for the mistake I will inevitably make to end the unexpected good fortune of his interest.

On day fifteen, it comes. But it's my mother's fault, not mine. There's a party at someone's house, nothing major, an afternoon get-together where the parents of the kid throwing it will be there and everything. The thing is, it'll be the first party I've ever been to with a boyfriend. I've already obtained permission to go: it's so important to me that I asked my mother about it before I was sure I was even invited. So I don't mention it again until the morning of.

My mother erupts. She yells that I'm inconsiderate, I don't know how hard she works, how incredibly much she does for me, how tired she is of my demands. It isn't fair; more than that, it's incomprehensible. The only thing my going to the party would interfere with is her predetermined idea of how the afternoon should unfold: me in my bedroom doing homework; her polishing the floors for the millionth time that week (my dad and I joke that she's having a steamy affair with Mr. Clean), checking in occasionally to see if I need a snack, while simultaneously preparing a big supper, too big, for the three of us. No one could blame me if I ran out the door and went to the party in spite of her. I'd be back by ten. She'd be wrapped up in her bedclothes by then, denying that the fight, the party, the whole glitch in her day ever happened. My father hates it when she and I go ballistic, and he's already taken off in the car. But unfortunately, I've erupted too. I've been crying for an hour — what is *wrong* with her? — and my face has swollen up like a kernel of that putrid pink popcorn they sell in boxes. My eyes are practically Krazy-glued shut. So there's no way I can go anywhere. The next day, I find out that another girl, a so-called friend, got together with my so-called boyfriend at the party. The day after that someone comes up to me and says, "You shouldn't try to talk to Jamie anymore. I just thought I'd let you know." And that's the end of that.

My mother gets wind of my status as a dumpee, and she gives me a long, heartfelt letter. "Any boy too stupid or immature or blind to know what a beautiful, brilliant, adorable young woman you are is not worth having," she writes. "In spite of the fact that you deserve nothing but the best, to be treated like a queen, I know you will probably have to experience a lot of pain in your life before you find what you're looking for, and I wish I could spare you from it. I wish I could take all the hurt for you instead."

I decide to keep a log of the mother-Melanie fights; even Mr. Martin seems to have abandoned uncertainty in favor of cold, hard data. We've been performing experiments lately, and although I'm as hopeless at them as I am at anything else to do with physics, my lab partner Lisa's are things of beauty. Their methodical, multicolored neatness, their perfectly underlined subsections and flawlessly tidy margins, inspire me. If I can find a pattern to the arguments with my mother, nail down the How, Where, and When of each one (if not the Why), maybe I can figure out how to avoid them, or at least impose a little order on the chaos they leave in their wake. As Mr. Martin wrote on the board today, *Disorder has a natural tendency to increase.*

Nothing happens for days. When the fight does come, it's only a minor skirmish, and it's over before my dad has a chance to turn the key in the ignition. But it's definitely in the realm of the noteworthy, and my heart pounds as I run up the stairs to make my first entry. I feel vindicated, somehow; I'd been starting to think the fights were all in my head. I guess this must be how Dr. Frankenstein felt when his monster first opened its eyes.

Fight Log, Entry #1

SUMMARY OF FIGHT: She accuses me of tearing apart all the work she does around the house without a thought to the million things she does for me every day.

FIGHT SPECIFICS
    Location: living room
    Duration: approximately 3 minutes
    Witnesses: the cat (for the first 10 seconds, before
        it ran away and hid)
    Time: 4:40 p.m.
    Catalyst: jacket left (by me) on the floor—temporarily!
        —as I ran to answer the phone

MAIN POINTS MADE
    Mom: She works like a slave. I treat her as such.
    Me: She is not reasonable. I am trying my best to live
    by her oppressive standards of neatness even though it

is against my true, more artistic nature. I should just move out.

Note: More colorful language (on both sides) was used to make these points.

METHOD OF TERMINATION: I ran up to my room and slammed the door. Offending jacket left behind. Dinner was served at around 6:00 p.m. without further incident.

Resolution: None

Conclusions: ???

At first, the Fight Log cheers me up quite a bit. For one thing, it gives me incentive to make earlier exits from the battlefield, since I can't wait to run up to my room and write down the more notable gems. By the third fight I've added a "Key Phrases" section, and that becomes my favorite part of the enterprise, though I'm not sure how much it furthers the scientific investigation. The top three hits on the current Key Phrases chart are, in order, "I have a million things to do," "Don't you care about me at all?," and "What's the matter with you?"

My entries make it sound like the fights are a big joke, and sometimes they are. Even before the log, my mother and I would often end an argument by staring at each other for a blank minute—maybe something like the phone ringing would have broken our stride—and then we'd suddenly crack up, both of us laughing and crying and apologizing.

The trouble is, not all of them are like that. When the big ones come, they hit hard. And they hurt. And I think that every time we have one, both of us shrivel up a little bit inside.

My mother was eighteen when she had me, just a year older than I am now. Her story is that she and my father got married sixteen months before I was born. But I know the wedding was only four months before. I found this out by snooping through her souvenir boxes, where she'd hidden their marriage certificate.

In those early days, my father says, he had to teach her how to do everything around the house. When she wanted to make instant coffee, she put milk in the kettle. And she cried, he told me, for the entire first month of their married lives.

From the moment I was born, my mother's life must have been like a never-ending racetrack, circling around me. The ten years I skated were the worst. Both of us at the arena by six in the morning. School for half a day. Back to the arena. Home for dinner. Arena again. Food provided; homework supervised; multiple changes of clothes picked out, lugged around, laundered, and put away again. Coaches consulted and, because I wasn't training quite full-time, constantly reassured; teachers spoken to, also reassured, about work missed in the half-day I was at the arena. My mother and I bounced from one place to the other, from one half-life to the other, like India-rubber balls. The only constant was each other.

Now that I'm no longer skating, my mother has time for a job, though most of the money she makes goes toward paying off our huge skating debts. At the moment, she sells shoes to a clientele consisting chiefly of little old ladies. I picture these ladies smiling in their kitchens, breaking in their sensible-but-stylish new shoes, basking still in the warmth of my mother's kindness. Once she's home, she has nothing but impatience for us.

Fight Log, Entry #15
Screw the format, I'm tired of it. It doesn't help, anyway. Nothing helps.

All I was doing was trying to be nice, trying to do something nice for her. So I decided I'd make dinner. Nothing special, just spaghetti. Pretty hard to burn down the house making that, right? And she freaked out. Came in and caught me at it (I wanted to have it all ready before she got home, bread and candles and everything) and said I was making a mess, I was undoing everything she'd done, and didn't I know she'd been on her feet for ten hours? And then I said it: *Don't be such a bitch.* Of course, she went nuts. I felt so bad. I tried to stop myself from talking, I knew it would just make things worse, but I kept wanting explain the difference between saying someone is a bitch and saying someone is *being* a bitch. But she kept going out of the room and then storming back in to unleash more pain and venom. So I got mad again and this time I called her something even worse, a *crazy* bitch. I honestly thought her face was going to burst open this time, and maybe my head and my heart and this whole freakshow of a house along with it.

Lately, when I close my eyes at night, it's not the elevator prisoners I see; I haven't been paying much attention to the outside world. Instead, it's things about my mother that rush in on me—the fights, naturally, but lots of other things, too. Like the time she was driving like hell on wheels to get me to a skating competition I was late for. We were in some strange city, and she was sick—we never found out with what. She was sweating, and a rash was breaking out all over her body and face. She ran three red lights in a row, and we got to the competition on time. I fell twice during my program, on elements that should have been easy for me. But my mother didn't say anything bad afterward. She told me I was the most beautiful skater in the competition, the same as she always did, and I know she believed it.

My first year of university, I'm a year younger than almost everyone else. My parents stick around the campus for a week, reluctant to say good-bye, until I practically have to chase them away. For a long time, I call my mother every few days. Gradually, though, I open up a door inside me for the new person who wants to get out, and I begin to have the best year of my life. The calls to my mom go down to once a week, on Sundays. The only log of their passing is my monthly phone bill.

The waters of our dissent, for now, are calm. But they'll never be still. Three months from now, Christmas Day, will see me striding down my parents' street with a half-packed suitcase in my hand, determined to catch the next bus back to university because of something she said. My father drives up behind me, telling me to cut the hysterics and come back for the dinner my mother spent the whole day preparing. If you ask me ten years on what the fight was about, I won't have a clue. But I'll remember the cold winter bite on my bare legs, the freezing of the tears around my eyes, the way the house smelled of turkey and oranges and Mr. Clean when I stepped back in through the front door.

IF YOU CAN'T BE GOOD

NANCY LEE

Twelve

IT BEGAN WHEN I STILL FELT LIKE A GIRL. My mom and I were living with my grandparents, and while they were away in China, she and I developed the habit of circling through the house every night before bed. We carefully checked each door and window in an effort to guard against intruders, the predatory men who spent their days luring children with candy, calling teenage girls towards slowing vans. My mom had nightmares of these men stealing me away, pulling me onto buses or trains, stuffing me in trunks.

Each night, as my mom checked the latch on the kitchen window, I imagined these men for myself, pictured scruffy, muscly vagrants leaving finger smears on our window ledges as they peered inside. I guessed that an angry fist, a heavy boot could easily break that thin pane of glass, the old locks on my grandparents' doors. I knew that if a man did try to snatch me from the street, if, in a grocery store, someone put a gun to my head, my cautious mother, a statuesque but soft-spoken woman, had no super-human powers of rescue, no bag of magic tricks, no real means of keeping me safe.

Thirteen

High school. On the blank canvas of new surroundings, I painted myself as exuberant and outspoken, covered the polite, bookish portrait I'd presented all through grade school. My best friend was a pretty, chatty girl named Tina who sat beside me in home economics. There was a boy, too. Jason. He was from England, which intrigued me because I had lived there as a child. Tina knew Jason's phone number; she and I sang it out every time we passed him in the hall. He didn't seem annoyed. Tina snuck him my number in a folded note, and soon after, through the hollow tunnel of my grandparents' phone, I heard him say my name.

My mom had forbidden me to speak to boys. After that first call, I raced to the phone whenever it rang, my nerves prickling as I grabbed the receiver. If she or my grandparents happened to be in the room, I'd pretend Jason was a girl, make my voice giggly and frivolous. It wasn't long before my mom picked up the downstairs extension and caught Jason mid-sentence. "Who are you talking to?" she demanded. The bark of her voice and the clamor as she slammed down the phone made me hot with embar-rassment. I babbled excuses before saying good-bye.

At the dinner table that evening, my mom was mute

with disapproval. She ignored me when I asked a question about the food we were eating. This was how she punished me, by withdrawing, leaving me in emotional isolation for hours, days until I repented. Her tactic was usually successful, but this time it backfired. Jason and I started eating lunch together at school, held hands in the hall; he was easy to talk to. I called him whenever my mom was busy with something or out of the house. I taught myself the difference between being allowed and being able.

My mom's edicts centered around one basic rule of conduct: Do nothing to shame your family. This was the Chinese way. My mom had been born in China. Though I grew up with the North American dream of adolescence—boyfriends, popularity, drugs, and alcohol—her youth was marked by a treacherous refugee boat ride across the Yangtze River and an agonizing deliberation over eating an apple or a banana, her first experience of fruit. "I wish I had chosen the banana," she often said, her voice heavy with regret, even though apples and bananas were consumed every day in our house. There were black-and-white photos of my mom at dances, but in them she danced with her brother and sisters. There were other photos of her with a boyfriend, but she was older in those, out of school and tutoring English. By the time she traveled to Wales to become a nurse, she was nineteen, an adult.

My mom was relieved when I brought home a permission form for the sexuality component of my grade eight guidance class. Someone else would explain everything. Though she worked as a nurse, sex was never mentioned in our home. Direction was given in abstract ways. If we were walking down the street together and saw a young teenage couple, my mom would say, "That girl is too young to have a boyfriend." Sixteen or seventeen seemed the acceptable age for an interest in boys; getting a boyfriend just before graduation, as it always played out on TV, was ideal. Girls who didn't wait, who had boyfriends before the maturity of near-adulthood, "got into trouble." Sex, my mom implied, was a treacherous slope for the young and curious.

The day of my first "date," I told my mom I was going to the library, then took the bus to Jason's. His mother worked in a lab all day; we had the place to ourselves. When I arrived, the emptiness and quiet of the apartment felt intimidating but liberating. I had never been alone with a boy. With our first nervous brush of skin, our first startling kiss, I saw, like a flare of bright light behind my closed eyelids, what all the trouble was about. Beyond the immediate adventure of being desired, the curious novelty of a boy's body so close to mine, I discovered something even richer and more heady: an intoxicating sense of power and independence. No one could tell me not to do this; no one controlled how my own body responded.

Fourteen

The distance that having a secret boyfriend put between my mom and me widened to a chasm. I became solitary and moody, participating only grudgingly in family meals. I moved across the hall from the bedroom I had shared with my mom, into the guest room, and covered my walls with posters of David Bowie and New Wave bands. I locked my bedroom door, sealing myself off from my family as soon as I got home.

Out of the house, I was ecstatic. I hung out downtown with friends or with Jason, scouring the import record store or standing around the food fair at the mall. I had begun experimenting with hair and fashion. The bands I liked wore outrageous outfits, streaked their hair purple and pink. I took scissors to my clothes, tore holes in all my tights and jeans. At school, I became infamous as the hyper chick who dressed weird — a reputation I relished.

I learned to move quickly in and out of the house, answering my mom's interrogations with the least amount of information.

"Where are you going?"

"Downtown."

"With who?"

"Some friends."

"What friends?"

"From school."

My mom would stand with her hands on her hips, a helpless look on her face as I rushed out the back door. "Be home by dinner!" she called after me.

But hanging out required spending money. I begged my mom to let me get a job. She refused, until my uncle offered me work at his donut shop as an evening janitor. The wage was insulting, even to a fourteen-year-old, but it was enough to buy records, magazines, and cigarettes.

"How are you doing in school?" my mom asked repeatedly.

"Great," I told her.

I knew she needed positive reports to take back to the family, who were even more alarmed than she that I had pierced my own ears and taken to decorating my clothes with safety pins. I could tell from the strain in her voice when she spoke with my grandparents that she was trying to convince them I was in a passing rebellious phase. She said the word "punk" with a forced laugh, as if it were a harmless fad like "bell-bottom" or "Hula Hoop." She made an effort to understand, sometimes pointing at pictures in magazines or things on TV and asking me, "Is that punk?"

Then my report card came out. I hadn't done homework since getting my job; I'd started skipping classes to avoid quizzes and assignments. Except for choir and drama, all of my As and Bs had become C-minuses. I armored myself against my mom's inevitable tirade. What I hadn't prepared for was the slouch in her body as she read the computer-generated page, the drawn and shaky trail of her hand down the column of grades. I launched into my speech: I hated my teachers; the gifted program I was in was too hard; I wanted to transfer out and join my friends in the regular stream.

"Just tell me you'll try harder," she said, her voice thin and defeated. She turned the page as if there might be better news on the other side. She sighed. "What if I pay you?" Her face was pale, as it sometimes looked after too many night shifts in a row. And though I felt guilty as the source of her unhappiness, I was enticed by the possibility of earning more money.

"A hundred dollars for every A," she said. "Fifty for every B. Like it's your job."

We had entered a new phase: negotiation.

As a child, I'd been very attached to my mom. I suffered stomachaches when she left for work and even phoned her at the hospital in the middle of the night to make sure she was there. She'd come home after a night shift, and, forgoing sleep, make us breakfast, then get me dressed and take me to the park to feed the ducks. As I got older, she took me to Christmas parties and baby showers. If friends invited her to a movie, she brought me along.

Both of us loved to read and eat in bed, and often we'd retreat from the blare of my grandparents' television, snacks in hand, to the quiet lull and bedside lights of our room. We shared a bedroom for so long that I'd memorized the sounds of her chewing orange wedges as I fell asleep.

Even as I lived my veiled adolescent life, I still sought this closeness with my mom. Sometimes I climbed into her bed to lie beside her while she read, and she would pat my teased, streaked, partially shaved head of hair. She talked to me softly when I cried over fights with friends or injustices at school, her everyday sternness yielding to gentle reassurance. I reveled in these moments, soaked up the comfort she was willing to give, yet thought nothing of turning down her suggestions of going out for ice cream or seeing a movie. I was pulled between the safety of childhood and the excitement of the adult world. The adult world won out every time.

My friends had begun pilfering alcohol from their

parents' stashes, buying pot and hash on the street. The first time I got stoned, I felt as if the sides of my throat were closing in. I had to escape the airlessness of Jason's apartment and step out onto the balcony, make a conscious effort to breathe. I imagined passing out and being rushed to the hospital, the shock on my mom's face when she found me there.

Fifteen

Jason and I broke up after I became interested in another boy. And another, and another. I had discovered a teen nightclub downtown and spent every Saturday afternoon getting ready for a night of dancing to imported club music. The kids I met there came from all over the city. Some of them commuted from rich neighborhoods, others had run away from group homes, some spent their nights on the street. All of us learned to lounge on the sidewalk and ask passersby for spare change, to linger outside the liquor store until a sympathetic adult took our handfuls of coins and went in to buy booze for us.

I dressed provocatively, imitating celebrities who had turned lingerie into streetwear. I changed my hair color from week to week. My grandparents gave up trying to correct my behavior and now scolded my mom whenever I did or said something that displeased them. My mom, whose height had always made her look strong and commanding, now seemed smaller as she stood, her shoulders curling forward with a permanent weariness.

My grades improved, but the demands of my social life were increasing, and I was often sleep-deprived and cranky.

I decided to go on the Pill to eliminate one source of worry in my life. I wanted to tell my mom. Partly I hoped she would see that I was responsible, not a foolish girl who would "get into trouble." Partly I was tired of hiding from her. I sat beside her on the couch and flipped through the telephone book, knowing it would draw her attention.

"What are you looking for?" she asked. She sat with her legs crossed at the knee, the TV remote balanced on the curve of her thigh.

"The number for the free clinic," I said as casually as I could. "I'm going on the Pill."

"What for?" Her voice was clipped; she turned and stared at the television.

I faked a laugh. "What do you think?"

She stayed silent and picked up the remote; the TV flicked from channel to channel. I hated that we communicated as if the truth were some kind of last resort.

Later that year I dated a boy with a jealous disposition and a raging temper. At first, he sulked and shouted; then he grabbed me during arguments, gripping my arm if I tried to walk away. Twice he pushed me hard enough that I fell down. One night, drunk at a party, he accused me of not loving him and punched me in the face. I felt a sudden lightness as my feet left the ground; I crashed into an antique credenza, knocking my head hard against the wood. As soon as I could stand, I left. The next day, I received my first delivery of long-stemmed roses, red velvet cups in a bed of baby's breath. I read the card, then pushed it and the roses into the garbage. My mom stood stunned at the kitchen sink. She dropped the vegetables she was washing and wiped her hands on a dishtowel. "What are you doing?" She had left the tap running; water gurgled in the drain. Before I could stop myself, I said, "He hit me." I braced for the lecture that would start, "How could you be so stupid?" Instead, my mom said something that squeezed the breath out of me and drove me upstairs to my bed, where I covered my face with a pillow: "Your father used to send flowers after he hit me."

She and I almost never talked about my father. I rarely thought of him except to be thankful he was no longer in our lives. He was a violent alcoholic, and my mom had left him when I was three. For years after, when she was especially mad at me, she'd say, "You're just like your father." Her pronouncement always made me cry and she'd immediately feel guilty, struggle to calm and console me. This mention of my father was different. Her way of saying "You're just like your mother" surprised us both.

Things changed slowly between my mom and me. She no longer grilled me about where I was going and whom I was going to see, but started to ensure I had enough money to last through the evening and get back home. As Tina and I made our way out of the house, she'd call, "Take care of each other. And if you can't be good, be careful." When we got home late—Tina staying at my house because her own home situation was unbearable—my mom would be waiting up. She'd cook food for us or warm up leftovers from dinner, sit and listen while Tina and I talked through the evening's events. There was something soothing about those late-night meals. My mom didn't say much; we often forgot she was there. But after the pulsing, smoke-filled haze of the dance club, the stumbling antics of drunk and stoned friends, the melodrama of careless flirtation and gossip— the quiet hum of the kitchen, the smell of hot food, the glow of the porch light in the darkness of our neighborhood made me happy to come home.

Things at my high school had become complicated. The student population was made up of metalheads and jocks, girls who were or behaved like cheerleaders and wanted to grow up to be stay-at-home moms. My increasingly eclectic taste in clothes, my weird music and hairstyles were less than appreciated. People shouted "Freak!" as I walked through the halls, threw food at me in the cafeteria. I decided to transfer to a more liberal school on the west side of the city. My mom supported my decision, saying, "If it's a better school, you should go." I promised myself I'd study harder, go to all my classes.

Sixteen

My next boyfriend, Sean, was a tall, sullen boy who lived with his grandparents. The bus ride to his house was two hours across town and after his grandparents suggested I stay the night instead of traveling home alone, I phoned my mom and told her I'd be sleeping over. She didn't protest.

My mom tried her best to treat me as an adult. On my dresser, she found a photo of some friends and me at a party, all of us with drinks and cigarettes in our hands.

"I used to smoke," she laughed. "You grow out of it."

She didn't tell me not to drink, but made me promise never to get into a car with someone who'd been drinking. She told me that no matter where I was, she'd pay my cab fare home.

I developed a series of painful urinary tract infections that year. My fourth time around, I received the wrong dose of antibiotics. My mom nursed me through a fevered night of vomiting and passing out. In the morning, she took me to the hospital, stayed with me in the emergency room, held my hand while the intern raised my feet into stirrups and did a pelvic exam. When we got home, she arranged blankets and pillows on the couch, lined up glasses of water and ginger ale on the coffee table, just as she had when I'd stayed home sick from grade school.

The situation with Sean was rocky. We spent most of our time fighting, then making up. My mom became used to my absence. My friends, irritated by my constant lateness and excuses, stopped inviting me out. One Sunday, Mother's Day, Sean and I were tangled in a fight that lasted all day and into the evening. I got home after midnight. I went to my mom's room to wake her and explain where I'd been, hoping to crawl onto her bed, have her reassure me that if Sean and I broke up, I'd be better off without him. But the door to her room was locked. I tapped softly.

"Go away," she said, her voice thick.

I heard muffled sounds of crying. I tried to coax her out of bed, said "I'm sorry" over and over, pushed against the door. Finally, I heard her get up and cross the room; the lock clicked. By the time I'd opened the door, she was already in bed again, her back to me.

I lay down behind her and put my arm over her still body. I whispered that I would make it up to her. "I know

I'm a horrible person," I said, and waited for her to forgive me. She lay there silent, unmoving. I whispered goodnight and went to my room.

A few days later, my mom and I arranged to meet after school. I bought flowers for her and took her out to dinner. She seemed happy. But somewhere inside myself, the residue of how thoughtless I'd been remained. It was as if all this time I'd been maintaining two selves—the bad person I was and the good person I wanted her to think I was. As long as I presented the good person to her, I'd thought, I still had the potential of being that person. But now we both knew the truth: there was only one version of me.

In April, Sean dropped out of school, and I started to miss classes to be with him. At first I skipped only the classes where the teachers didn't take attendance, then I moved on to skipping that required forged notes and creative explanations. Eventually, I missed entire days, Sean phoning the school in the morning and posing as my father. It never occurred to me that the school would know from my records that I didn't have a father.

I got home one of those afternoons and went to my mom's room to say hello; she was dressed to go out, her hair and makeup done, her coat beside her on the bed. She stood and demanded to know where I'd been. I started to tell her I'd been at school, but before I could finish, she reached out her hand and slapped my face.

"Stop lying," she shouted. She glared at me.

I froze with my mouth open, trying to remember the last time she'd hit me. I felt the rims of my eyes warm with tears.

"The school called." Her voice was hard and angry. "Your principal wants to see me in the morning. What am I supposed to say? I had to call into work and ask for a day off. Now I have to sit and listen while someone tells me what a poor student you are. Why do you do this to me? I give you everything, and this is how you repay me, by being stupid and irresponsible."

I started to sob, the side of my face still stinging. "You don't understand anything!" I screamed. "I hate that school!" This wasn't a lie; I was miserable at school and I missed my old friends, but I was also trying to draw out her sympathy, sidetrack her with my own unhappiness.

Her face remained cold, her voice low and brittle. "I've spent my whole life working hard so that you could have every opportunity. I am sick and tired of how ungrateful and selfish you are. You have no respect for anyone, not even yourself."

She snatched up her coat and purse and pointed at me. "I'm going out to dinner with the family. You don't leave this house for any reason." I obeyed.

The next morning, my mom and I sat silent in the school office. She'd worn a new suit and her best jewelry. Neither of us spoke. My ribs felt as though they were twisting inside me as we waited for the principal to call us in.

We sat down across from him, an earnest, balding man in a gray suit and gray tie. He smiled politely at my mom and she smiled back, bowing her head slightly. I could tell she was intimidated by his tidy brown office, his position of authority.

He started with pleasantries, but quickly got down to

business. "The bottom line is," he said with sigh, "your daughter has missed so many classes this year, she's on the verge of suspension. We take absenteeism very seriously here, and I think this situation warrants some measure of reprimand and redirection."

My mom nodded as she listened, fiddled with the rings on her fingers, made small noises of agreement in her throat. I chewed the insides of my mouth, prepared for her respectful apologies on my behalf, her pleadings that the school give me another chance.

She straightened in her chair and took a deep breath before speaking. "My daughter is very intelligent and independent." The firmness of her voice startled me. "She's very mature for her age, and she knows what she wants. If she's missed classes, it's because she's unhappy at your school."

Stunned, I looked quickly to the principal; his face had taken on an expression of unarmed surprise, his head cocked back so that his chin crumpled in folds. He brought his hand to his mouth and cleared his throat.

My mom continued, "Since the school year is almost over and my daughter is planning to transfer back to her old school, I don't see this as a problem."

I tried very hard not to smile.

The principal moved a few papers around on his desk, then mumbled something as he stood. He shook hands with my mom and thanked her for coming.

I said good-bye to my mom outside the school. The day was clear and bright, and she looked elegant in her tailored suit, her broach and rings winking in the sunlight. In heels, she was a few inches taller than I was. She hugged me, and I felt the warmth of her body, smelled the mix of her drugstore cosmetics and expensive perfume. As she drew away, she mustered a stern look and stared me straight in the eye. "Don't ever make me do that again," she said. I nodded. I stood on the corner and watched as she made her way down the street to the bus stop. At a certain distance, she no longer looked like my mother, but instead a graceful, anonymous woman walking through the city, her purse tucked neatly under her arm, her back straight, the clicks of her heels diminishing as she moved farther and farther away.

WHEREVER YOU ARE

PRISCILA UPPAL

I DON'T KNOW WHY I HAD TO BE THE GIRL in school without a mom. Maybe there were others, but if so, they did a better job of hiding it than I did. I mean, tons of teenagers had no dad, and there were many weekend dads, dads-of-the-moment, and stepdads. I knew people with stepmoms and real moms. But no mom? I was the only one who was motherless.

Mom, where were you?

★ ★ ★

I felt as if *unloved* was stitched on my school uniform like a crest. Warning, it signaled. This girl's own mother was unable to love her. This girl is no good. She has done something terrible. The doctor found a mark on her as a newborn and knew immediately it meant trouble.

Is there any hope, Doctor? I can hear my mother say,

clutching her purse, trying to avoid my deep-brown eyes as the man with the pale-green mask hung around his neck held me down on the cold, steel scale. *None. None at all. Best to go now. Make a new life. New babies elsewhere. You won't miss her. Trust me.* I was eight pounds, two ounces. Perhaps not heavy enough to keep her here.

But I missed her. I missed her when my friend Jessica's mother made pancakes and hashbrowns on the Saturday mornings I went over to watch cartoons, or when Tailin's mother took us to the movies on cheapo Tuesdays. Bryan's mother called out to him on the street as we boarded the bus not to forget his piano lesson after school. Peter's mother had *everyone* over one day to try out their family's new pool and diving board. She strung red and yellow balloons across the fence and gave everyone a kiss and a goodie bag filled with licorice and bubble gum on the way out. She had blonde hair, held back with two gold barrettes, and wore a purple scarf around her waist. She smelled like lily of the valley when she kissed my forehead.

My father made pancakes from a mix and swore whenever the smoke alarm went off because he'd left them in the frying pan too long while he read the newspaper. He liked cartoons but said they taught me bad manners. He looked into piano lessons, but even the cheapest student teachers from the arts academy were too expensive. *Besides,* he said, *smart girl like you, we'll need the money to send you to a real university.* When I showed him my goodie bag from the pool party, he called Peter's mother a *show-off.*

In grade eleven, Jade's mom let us drink beer and vodka coolers while we listened to rock and heavy metal in the basement. She didn't like us smoking but left us an ashtray anyway, so we wouldn't end up burning her carpet. She even let Jade *entertain* boys, which meant they could come and have a beer, too, but never late at night. When boys were there, Jade's mom would bring down chips and vegetables and dip and ask us a bunch of questions about school or our families. She meant well. *I don't think that social studies assignment is fair,* she said to me. *Asking you all to write about your family histories, like it's any of their business. Don't you worry, your father will get you out of it.* She said it in front of the biggest loudmouth at school, and the next day a bunch of smokers by the back door, inhaling quickly before the bell went off, asked me if it was true my mother was in jail. I shook my head and jogged to my locker.

Jade's mom took her to the doctor and put her on the Pill to help her acne. Jade hardly had any acne. Once she called me up horribly embarrassed. Her mother had taken a cucumber and shown her how to put a condom on it. *Because I won't be there when you get yourself into these situations,* she told Jade. *If you won't say no to a boy, at least I want you to know what to do.* I had no idea what to do. I didn't even like cucumbers. My father would never have said the word *condom* anywhere near me. If anyone had asked him, he wouldn't have been able to say for sure whether I'd ever been kissed.

Nor would he have interfered with a school project. He skipped PTA meetings and after-school plays and sports events. He never accepted the invitations of my friends' parents to go out for the evening or to carpool. Instead, he watched television long into the night and took on extra shifts at work. As long as my grades were high and I stayed out of *serious trouble* (which to him meant that I wasn't pregnant, a cocaine addict, or a suicide risk), my father saw no reason to *interfere* in my life. He didn't want anyone else to interfere in his. And certainly not the way my mother had. I wondered at times if he saw her in me. If he looked. Between the television and the newspaper, the bills and the appliances that always seemed to need fixing, I'm not sure my father saw much of me at all.

★ ★ ★

So, like, what happened to your mom? No matter how much I avoided the topic with new friends and their families, with new boyfriends and teachers and coaches, eventually the question would be asked. I had countless answers.

My Mother's Disappearance: Take One

My mother was once engaged to a very rich man. She was fond of him, but not in love. Then she met my father, and he dazzled her with his sensitivity and gorgeous green eyes. My mother broke off her engagement and married my father, and they had a beautiful baby girl. But the rich man went utterly mad without her. One day as she was watering our rose garden, a helicopter landed in the middle of our street, and a masked man jumped out and hauled her away. The rich man has not let her out of his sight since. Every once in a while I'm sure she tries to telephone me, but her efforts are always thwarted. The rich man's servants are obviously very smart and very loyal.

My Mother's Disappearance: Take Two

My mother was adopted, and after I was born she set out to find her biological parents. On safari in the jungles of Africa, where she had heard her real father was a doctor curing leprosy, she became very ill with a rare blood disease after drinking the local water. A man in the safari party carried her the final seventeen miles to the home of the doctor. Her father worked on her for seven full days and nights before she regained consciousness in his arms, his tears dripping onto her cheeks. When she recovered, she promised she would never leave him. She has since married the man who delivered her to her father, and they have thirteen adopted children.

My Mother's Disappearance: Take Twenty-Seven

She was swallowed by a killer whale on a trip to Marineland. Very tragic. Made all the papers. A local anchorwoman called me brave.

My Mother's Disappearance: Take One Hundred Fifty

My mother has been touring with an English punk band for the past seven years. She plays guitar and sings the lead. Her hair is in red dreads, and she loves paisley halter tops. She stays in high-class hotels and orders up fish and chips whenever she feels like it. She wears an expensive watch that shows three different time zones. She's never in the same place for more than a few days. No one ever asks her if she has children, because she looks so young. I get postcards. I can show them to you if you don't believe me.

My Mother's Disappearance: Director's Cut

My mother left one day and never came back. She didn't want to be found.

How could I tell my friends, my friends' parents, my teachers *that?* What kind of mother left her child because she didn't want her anymore? What kind of mother prepared lunch, put her daughter on the bus, kissed her husband good-bye on his way to work, brewed tea, and then packed her bags and boarded a plane to London's Heathrow Airport, with the option of several connecting flights from there? The airline and the credit card company sent us the bills. It was the first time, but certainly not the last, that I saw my father weep.

★ ★ ★

My father and I kept my mother's picture in the living room until I couldn't bear to stare at her face any longer. I locked the photo in her chest, the one she left filled with her old clothes. I often had the urge to try them on, especially a pair of silver pants with sequins that I didn't remember her ever wearing. But when I touched the pant legs, it was as if I were emptying them of her body, admitting she'd never return. I couldn't bear that either. *Where'd your mother go?* my father asked. *Her picture from the mantel, where is it?* I shrugged. *I really don't think she'd mind, do you?* My father phoned the pizza parlor to deliver our dinner. *I suppose you're right,* he said.

He kept their wedding album, white with silver end-papers, hidden in the filing cabinet in the basement where he stored decades of income tax forms. Once I'd discovered it there, I could sneak a peak whenever I liked. It wasn't the pictures themselves I was interested in. I knew what my father looked like with a beard and how my mother's top lip curled up higher on the left side when she smiled. What drew me were the pages themselves. There were the same number of them no matter how many times I opened the album, flipping past the calligraphic swirl of our last name on the cover. The pages could be counted on, though the people inside them couldn't.

Kodak Moments Fantasy Collection: Great New Parents Make Me Forget the Past

I have won my umpteenth award for excellence at school, and the principal has had enough of me dragging my schoolbag home to a silent, sad house. He has secretly contacted an adoption agency, weeding out parents not good enough to take care of *such a special, intelligent young woman* as myself. He has rejected thousands of applications from homemakers and architects, world travelers and small-town, honest, church-going ladies, women with armloads of children and women whose only dream is to have a girl to call their own. He's decided on a husband-and-wife team of retired Nobel Prize–winning chemists. They are very kind, and they can afford to send me to any university on the globe. I carry my schoolbag nervously over to their house. I have never been to this side of town before.

Their house has a veranda and a gazebo. A pool.

There's a cat called Marie. My new parents and I have fake by-invitation-only tea parties out in the sun. We play badminton, knocking the birdie back and forth over a net tied between two maples. I have a tent in which to sleep under the stars and a map of the constellations in my pillowcase. I am read to, even though of course I can already read. My new mother hugs me often *for no reason.* I slowly forget I was ever motherless. My new father says it's alright for me to forget my real father, too. I am so happy I can't refuse them. I receive a full scholarship to Harvard, and we move together to Boston.

Kodak Moments Fantasy Collection:
My Best Friend's Mother Legally Adopts Me

My best friend (insert name here) and I are eating waffles with extra-creamy butter and maple syrup. Our sleeping bags, unrolled, are like giant tongues hanging out, spent after hours of us laughing too hard. We are going to the zoo today. We love summer. The previous night we were allowed to rent two movies, eat a bag of popcorn and a whole box of macaroons, put on red lipstick and blue eye shadow, and stay up as long as we could.

My best friend's mother is beautiful. She has the most wonderful (insert color here) hair and the most appealing (insert nationality here) accent. She thinks it's absurd not to give her daughter the sister *she would choose herself.* Before heading out to the zoo, as we are wiping off our eye shadow and tying our sneakers, she announces that the papers have arrived. *The papers that will make you sisters legally,* she says, gazing anxiously in my direction. I trade glances with my best friend, who is practically bursting with joy. I scream and run into their arms, my new mother and new sister nearly crushing me with love. At the zoo, we ride a camel, squished together between the humps. We wave at the camera.

Kodak Moments Fantasy Collection: I Meet My Soulmate Mother through a TV Game Show

Three ladies compete for the chance to take home a wonderful teenage girl: me. Shielded by a curtain, I am able to ask each of them questions in front of an audience.

Me: Possible Mother #1, if I was arrested for shoplifting some junk earrings from a department store, what would you do?

PM #1: I'd come and pick you up from the store and convince the police officers and security staff to keep the offence off your record, considering how cheap the jewelry was.

Me: Possible Mother #2, same question.

PM #2: I wouldn't yell at you in front of the security staff, but when I came to pick you up you would know I was disappointed in you. I would take you to court if needed, but I'd be more concerned about why you stole the jewelry. I'd want to know why you felt low enough to do something like that, so that I could help you feel better.

(The audience applauds loudly for Possible Mother #2. She smiles with satisfaction.)

Me: Okay, I'm going to ask you all the same question, starting with Possible Mother #3. Why do you want to be my mother so badly?

PM #3: My own mother was horrible to me as a child,

and I'd like the chance to make a deserving girl like you happy.

Me: #1?

PM #1: I am unable to have children myself. My greatest joy would be a daughter to talk to in my old age.

Me: #2?

PM #2: I think fate brought me here today. I believe we are meant to be together. I have always wanted a daughter, but not just any daughter: a daughter like you that a mother could really be proud of.

(Audience jumps to their feet, applauding. Possible Mother #2 comes out from behind the curtain, and we embrace as if we were born embracing. Colored balloons and confetti fall from the ceiling.)

Kodak Moments Rewind Reel:
It Was All a Terrible Misunderstanding

It's the end of my shift at the drugstore, where I have a part-time job. After this, I'm going off to meet my new boyfriend at the movies. A woman who looks vaguely familiar walks up to me just as I'm locking the doors for the night.

Can I …? she stumbles.

We're closed until eight a.m. Sorry, I tell her.

No, I don't want to buy anything. I want my daughter.

Does she work here? I ask.

She nods vigorously as she digs frantically in her purse for something. I notice her eyes are full of tears.

I am the last one here, I say softly. I'm sorry. *You must have missed her.*

I miss her very much, she replies, producing a finger-worn birth certificate with my name on it.

I back away, shocked. *You can't be my mother,* I tell her. *My mother left me.*

No, she replies, shaking her head emphatically. *I was forced to leave you. Our country was in danger, and I worked for the government in a secret unit. I was one of their most valuable operatives, as I can speak fourteen languages fluently. If I had refused, they would have kept my family away from me. My weekly letters to you and your father, I found out recently, were never delivered. I am now free to return and make up for all the time I've spent away from you, the person I love most in the world.*

Hand in hand, my mother and I set off to meet my new boyfriend. We all skip the movie and head home to join my father for a welcome-home dinner.

Photo-Album Reality

There are no pictures of my mother and me in the wedding album. Or any album in the house. She has chosen a life without me. I have no choice.

She wasn't there, of course, when we realized what had happened. When the police phoned back to tell us about the plane ticket and the empty bank accounts. My father took out two bowls and two spoons and a full carton of vanilla ice cream. How we ate it. Every last spoonful.

★ ★ ★

I thought my friends were spoiled and ungrateful. They complained if they didn't get what they wanted for Christmas, if their allowance wasn't raised, or some outrageous request (like spending an unsupervised weekend with a boyfriend or girlfriend) was refused. I figured their mothers must be sick of their whining too, but every time I went over to their houses or to school plays or soccer games, there were those same mothers—proud of a boy who couldn't get higher than a C in any subject, tickled pink with a girl who'd been caught giving a blow job to some senior in the gymnasium equipment room. I couldn't believe that their love was so *unconditional*. What was so special about those kids? I had an A-plus average, an MVP award for girls' basketball, many friends. The teachers were crazy about me, if a little concerned by the sadness evident in my black clothes and nail polish and my writing assignments. Sasha could barely work out her lunch money for the week. Danielle slept with anyone who told her she was pretty. Kassy crashed her mother's brand-new car during spare period after smoking a joint. It was completely nonsensical.

Moments I Could Have Used a Mother: Age 11

I am buying my first bra. My father has given me his Sears card and a note authorizing me to use it along with his phone number. I run my hands over the different Wonderbra packages, the photographs of women with their chests stuck out as if breasts were the most natural things in the world. Mine are small and hard as olive pits. I'm afraid that people will think I'm a pervert if I stare at the boxes too long, so I grab two off the rack, and sign the Sears card receipt as quickly as possible. The saleswoman is so busy flirting with a male customer that she barely glances at me.

When I get home and try on the bras, I discover I have bought size 40C. My doll's head fits in the cups. My breasts most certainly do not. I'm afraid my father will be angry, so I cut part of the cups off and shorten the straps and sew the material back together by hand. My bra is snapped by a boy the first day I wear it, and it falls apart underneath my shirt. I pretend I'm ill and come home. I tell my father I'm still too young to wear a bra, and he looks relieved.

Moments I Could Have Used a Mother: Age 12

I'm at tennis camp, practicing my double-handed backhand and perfecting my smile on the redheaded twenty-two-year-old instructor, when I notice my panties feel damp. I ignore it, since I've gotten used to this feeling coming over me when the instructor holds my elbows and curves his hips around my waist to show me what he calls *proper form*. When we break for lunch, I choose a spot on the grass beside him, and I tell him boldly that I know a girl who is already screwing boys in grade eight, the grade I'm in. He laughs. *You've got something on your shorts,* he says, turning to the female instructor to share his bag of chips.

I look down. My shorts are dotted brown. I ask to go home. He knows I'm just a little girl. It's my first period, and he knows I'm going home to put on a pad. I can barely make out which one is my house, I'm crying so hard, whacking my racket over and over against the curb.

Moments I Could Have Used a Mother: Age 14

This girl named Rebecca calls me Paki and spits in my face. I have no idea what she's talking about. I've never heard of Pakistan. We've never even had a test on it.

My father was born in India. My mother was born in Brazil. *They'd like all of us to leave,* my father yells after I tell him what happened. *See how happy they'll be if we do. Then they'll have no one to blame but themselves.*

Moments I Could Have Used a Mother: Age 16

He's twenty-four. He comes to pick me up from the school dance in his car, and we go back to his place. He lives in a rented house with two roommates who are, he tells me, jealous he's found himself *such a pretty young thing.* He lights white candles in his bedroom, offers me a glass of wine, and presents me with a black silk nightgown with a bit of lace at the breasts. He knows I'm a virgin, and he wants me to *be comfortable.* I'm scared, but I think he's cute. He's French, too, and he's cool. My friends all tell me so. *You're so beautiful you ought to be illegal,* he says.

It hurts. The first time hurts. But he goes slowly, and we do it again later. Then again. It starts to hurt a little less.

In six weeks he will break up with me in his car after we exchange Christmas gifts. He's found someone his own age. It will be many years before I do.

★ ★ ★

If I brought home nothing but A-plus report cards forever, I'd still have no mother. If I became the most popular, sought-after girl in school, I'd still have no mother. If I won hundreds of scholarships to university, earned my degree in a single year, married some high-school sweetheart, and raised three gorgeous children while managing to shoot to the top of the *New York Times* best-seller list and keep our love flame alive, I'd still have no mother. I couldn't trade or barter for someone else's. I couldn't rent one for the day or take out an ad in the newspaper. No matter what successes or triumphs I earned, I could never earn a mother. I was motherless. Less something *I* might have needed.

I'm afraid of girls. *You're my best friend,* one will say. The next day: *You were my best friend yesterday but not today. Okay? Get over it.* Girls are always wondering what boys think of this and that. Of them. If you are in the way of the boy (or man) she wants, a girl will pass you by. Without a second glance. Until, of course, she *needs* you again.

I suspect one day my mother might need me too.

I miss you, Mom, wherever you are.

Do you miss me?

IN THE SILENCE THAT SPEAKS

SUE GOYETTE

MY MOTHER RESCUED ME ONCE when I was four. It was winter, and my nose was filled with the cold, wet-wool smell of my scarf and mitts. The drifts of snow were high, over my head, and I'd been outside long enough for my toes to feel like they were burning. It was time to go in. As I stood at the door of our apartment building, I was taken over, seized by an urge to lick the doorknob. Maybe it looked bright and inviting in a brass-lollipop way, or maybe I was thirsty and the shine of the sun on the knob made the handle look like water, but whatever the reason, the urge became irresistible and I stretched my tongue out, briefly tasting the cold metal before realizing I was stuck. Filled with panic, I screamed open-mouthed, in the *ahh* way like when the doctor peered down my throat, holding my tongue flat with a wide Popsicle stick. I shuffled my feet backward as the door finally opened and my mother came out. She poured warm coffee over my tongue until it loosened its grip. I screamed again then, not at the thought of how my tongue had almost been ripped out but at the awful taste in my mouth, the bitterness lingering until I spit myself dry. My first sip of coffee. My mother hurried me inside, stepping over the heaped snow in her bright turquoise slippers. I could see them even in the dark hallway, flip-flopping quickly up the stairs ahead of me.

★ ★ ★

My mother was the Tawny Owl in my Brownie pack. She would squat on her haunches with the best of them, twit-twit-twooing with Brown Owl and Wise Owl around the papier-mâché toadstool on the green bathroom mat in the middle of the gym floor as we performed one of the many ceremonies our pack had perfected. She'd spend long nights cutting out the paper for the craft we were going to make the following week on our kitchen table with her pinking shears. She was creative, which made her different from other people's mothers. Her creative way of dressing was one of the reasons I shrank from her in public. The special hat she wore in spring looked like something pink exploding on her head, and she dressed entirely in green on St. Patrick's Day. One September, she spent hours decorating a back-to-school-after-summer cake with cut-out pictures of pencil cases and binders. The kids I knew ate Cheese Whiz and crackers after school; we had to peel paper rulers off our food. Other stay-at-home mothers seemed normal. They baked regular brownies, made plain, round pancakes, and kept busy visiting other mothers who did the same things. My mother read. Reading sounds like a calm activity, but she read with a fierce hunger, tearing through a book in an afternoon. She loved murder mysteries, horror, and science fiction. Our coffee table wasn't stacked with the romance novels my friends' mothers read, or magazines like *Reader's Digest,* but with books that had gruesome covers: corpses dripping blood, fanged monsters, a clawed hand scraping menacingly down a wall. Those kinds of books spiced up her life, my mother would say, tossing the latest one onto the table. My friends would squeal when they saw them, then look at me differently, as if I was the giant green alien and the covers of the books displayed my family's portraits.

We lived in a small town on the outskirts of Montreal. Most of the books in our local library were written in French, but my mother had found a library in Ontario that would send us English books by mail, and in every box there'd be a selection card for ordering the types of books you wanted to receive in the next shipment. My mother would study the card like a menu, as if this time she was considering trying something new, but inevitably she'd tick off the boxes beside "Murder mystery" and "Science fiction." I, more adventurous, was making my way down the column of categories systematically, taking a turn reading something from each one. "Historical nonfiction" nearly killed me, until my mother told me that I didn't have to finish every book I started, that it was okay to give up on something if it was sending me into a deep sleep or a coma.

After that, I read at the same speed she did, voraciously zipping through Nancy Drew mysteries and then S.E.

Hinton novels, books about girls in trouble, about families, books with characters I cared about and worried over. I would read quickly through their crises to get them back to safety. Books became my life. It was like Christmas when a new box arrived. My mother would always leave it for me to open when I got home from school, wait while I pulled out all of my books before she took out hers. Ramona and Barbara, friends who'd come home with me after school, would wait till my mom left the room, then pick up her books with utter distaste. "Who," they'd ask disdainfully, "would want to read this?" I'd shrug and agree. "Disgusting," I'd say about the voluptuous women on the sci-fi covers, their flimsy dresses barely covering breasts just panting to pop out. But I'd say it quietly, because my mother was usually hovering around somewhere, pasting glitter to toilet paper rolls with my two younger sisters, outlining their hands on paper and then drawing them into birds. I always made sure Ramona and Barbara left before suppertime, when my father got home. The aliens on the covers of my mother's books were one thing, but my father was a whole other story.

Barbara's mother volunteered at our school, but she'd be at home when Barbara and her brother got there, holding out a plate of freshly baked cookies or carrot sticks and dip, just like a picture in a magazine. Their house was spotless. My mother wore the same slacks and sweater almost every day. It was easier, she'd say, than picking out something new. She watched TV and listened to her records. She'd bang pots along with a singer called Engelbert Humperdinck, a name my sisters and I would chant while he sang, pulling out the sound of it until we got to the "dink," then laughing uproariously. Another of her favorites was Tom Jones, who'd wail all afternoon, singing "Why, why, why?" as if my mother wanted to know as well. She didn't like cooking much. She Shake 'n Baked chicken, pork, anything she could. She'd make instant mashed potatoes and open cans of green beans or peas during the commercial breaks in *As the World Turns*, worried about whether Betsy and Steve would get caught having their affair. I thought my mother was crazy, and I'd try to talk Ramona into going to her house after school as often as I could.

Ramona's parents were never home. Her mother sold real estate. She wore skirts and blouses to work, frosted her lips with shimmer lipstick, and plucked her eyebrows into thin, fine arcs that gave her a look of gentle surprise. Her father rented out medical equipment, and Ramona and I would drink crème de menthe and dare each other to open his books, inspecting photographs of people with bizarre physical ailments that both fascinated us and grossed us out. We'd laugh, half in shock, as we looked at the section on penises and bums, our tongues stained green, our heads wobbly.

Ramona phoned me the day she started her period for the first time. She panicked at first, she told me, thought she was bleeding to death until she realized what was happening. Then she couldn't find any pads or tampons in her house. "Tell her to use Kleenex or a facecloth until you can get over there," my mother instructed, filling a grocery bag with some maxi pads. "Tell her to use cold water to wash her things. Make her a cup of tea."

One afternoon, Ramona came home and surprised her mother on the couch with their Japanese gardener. They were naked. Ramona called me that night, telling me in an almost hysterical whisper what had gone on when her father got home. The Japanese gardener was even shorter than we were, she reported, and his penis was like the one on page 56. Ramona's parents separated after that, and she stayed in the house with her father. All he did was bake pies, she'd complain. Every day there'd be a pie cooling on the counter that he'd urge her to eat. She was starting to feel sick about it all, she said. And she was getting fat.

Barbara's mother got up at five o'clock every morning to drive Barbara to figure-skating practice. But one day, while the three of us were playing Truth or Dare, Barbara confided to Ramona and me that her mother kept a glass of rum and Coke behind the blender all day, taking sips when she didn't think anyone was watching. After that, I spied on her whenever I was over there.

My parents didn't drink. My mother kept a bottle of sherry under the kitchen sink, but she'd take it out only when my grandparents visited. I ended up drinking the entire bottle myself one afternoon in grade nine, listening to music as I sobbed over a very embarrassing situation that had occurred at the school dance the weekend before. Drinking had become one of our forms of weekend entertainment. This particular incident involved me and a boy named Glenn and a small bottle of vodka and the lights going on during the Led Zeppelin song "Stairway to Heaven" and the entire school witnessing his hand up my shirt. My mother didn't notice the missing sherry, but she did notice that I didn't get out of bed the next day until noon. I came down, groggy and with a headache, to the heart-shaped pancakes she had left at my place at the table. They looked cold and soggy, and there was no way I could eat them.

★ ★ ★

One night when I was thirteen, my mother drove over to Barbara's house to pick me up. It was summer, but already too dark for me to walk home by myself. My mother turned up in her nightgown and robe, curlers in her hair. I was glad Barbara hadn't walked me out to the car and seen her dressed that way. I felt ashamed of her worn nightie, the faded flowers on it. I turned on the radio so I wouldn't have to talk, wouldn't have to answer the standard questions about what Barbara and I had done and whether or not I had eaten. As the deep voice of the radio announcer filled the car with the news that Elvis Presley had died, I heard my mother's breath catch. She pulled the car over and parked under a drooping weeping willow, one of many that lined the street. Elvis crooning "Love Me Tender" was velvet smoke that whirled around us and drifted out the open windows of the car up into the sky. My mother rested her head on the steering wheel and sobbed silently, her shoulders shaking. It was the first time I could remember seeing her cry. I wasn't sure what to do, whether I should reach out and touch her. It seemed like a private moment, something I knew nothing about. Finally, after the third song had played, I did reach out. I wanted to go. My mother looked at me, her eyes red, her breathing still ragged. Then she cleared her throat and drove us home. She was young when she started listening to Elvis, she told me, looking straight ahead into the night. She had loved him so much, she'd kiss her pillow pretending it was him. "But that was a long time ago," she said wistfully, looking up at herself in the rearview mirror. I left her to it, not really understanding that long look back.

★ ★ ★

When I was fourteen, my mother got a part-time job in the men's department at Eaton's, in the new mall on the highway outside of town. She spent her hours there folding dress shirts and making suggestions about accessories, the right color of tie, matching socks. She spoke French with a terrible accent, and she lived in fear of "being shopped" by one of the spies the store hired to check up on their staff. She had to remember to smile and to read the names on credit cards so she could use them when she wished her customers a nice evening.

My mother would leave for work just as I was getting home from school, and my job was to make supper for my father and two sisters. My father wasn't pleased to be left alone to eat casseroles with us every night. For the first time, I witnessed his temper without my mother there to act as a buffer. He'd whip his belt off when my youngest sister wasn't hungry, lash it close to her threateningly. "I work my ass off to put food on this table, and you will sit there and eat that food," he'd holler. I'd slip into my mother's role then, stand between him and my sister and dare him to do it again. I got hit and yelled at, but my sister was safe. As I faced him down, she'd slide off her chair and disappear.

At first I enjoyed the power that came with doling out the desserts, but I quickly longed for time to myself again, for my mother to be home and doing what she had always done. Some nights I wouldn't think much about my sisters. I'd cook dinner, then go hang out with my friends, to get out of the house and away from my father. We'd walk to the mountain across town or to the lake at the town's center. The lake was so polluted that rumor had it a dog had paddled in to get a tennis ball and developed rabies the next day. I'd drink beer or cider, smoke grass and hash. While my mother was ringing in sales, I dropped acid. My father wasn't an easy man, and we each handled that in our own ways.

Because my mother was always on the verge of being late for work, she'd leave me long notes, instructing me how to heat up the chili she had made, reminding me to feed the dog or take the ice cream out of the freezer for dessert. She'd sign the notes MOM!, with an exclamation mark, a happy face in the O's circle, and curly hair sprouting from the top of it like springs. I'd write her back. "I need tampons," I'd scrawl, or "I need five dollars for school," and it would be on the kitchen table for her in the morning. I was staying out later and later by then, and when I did get home, I headed for the basement right away, putting on headphones so I wouldn't hear the upstairs commotion of my family. I barely got up in time to catch my bus in the mornings, let alone talk to her.

We didn't get books in the mail anymore. My mom didn't have time to read, she said. I read books from the school library instead and wrote long poems about eternity and death in the silk-covered notebooks I bought at a head shop in Montreal. The store had a huge display of roach clips in the window, hash pipes, bongs, black-velvet posters, beads, incense. I wrote poems about karma and about Mark in my woodworking class, who had the sweetest crooked smile and the best faded jeans, ripped in a nonchalant way that was really hot. I sometimes left the poems lying around and my mother would gather them up. I had a way with words, she'd tell me after reading them. I began smoking cigarettes, first lying about it, then lighting one up in front of her, daring her to say something. After that, she would sometimes leave me packs of cigarettes on the kitchen table and lighters with my name printed on them, or my astrological sign. "You're so lucky," my friends would say. "Your mother is so cool."

At lunch, my friends and I would go down to the diner around the corner from our school. I had started hanging out mostly with guys by then, not liking the way girls were so two-faced with each other, talking about everyone behind their backs. Guys didn't give a shit about who wore what on which day or who was going out with who. They just wanted to party, listen to good music, and stay out as late as they could. The Labatt truck that delivered cases of beer to the bars in town always parked at the diner on Thursdays. Payday, we figured. Ross had discovered a way to open up the back of the truck without making too much noise, so every Thursday afternoon found us in a nearby field with a couple of stolen cases of beer. We'd drink until the dismissal bell, then hurry back to school to catch our buses home. We'd run across the parking lot, laughing at each other as we bumped into cars, struggling to stay upright.

The second time I saw my mother cry was on one of those Thursday afternoons. "You're plastered," she hissed, watching me try to untie my shoes as I fell into the wall. She was dressed for work, wearing her lipstick and her name tag. There was a casserole dish on the counter waiting to be put in the oven, and I had a blurred vision of the note, the smiley face, the instructions: "4:15 p.m. at 350°, stir in half an hour, supper at 5:00. Love MOM!" "You're ruining my plans," she said tearfully. "You're the only one I can count on."

I didn't care if I was ruining her plans. I had drunk four beer on an empty stomach, and Ross had broken the silent code of friendship by drunkenly asking me out. "You're ruining my plans," I retorted icily.

And then she said something in such a steely voice that I immediately sobered. "Don't you dare speak to me in that tone. I am your mother."

I heard myself answer her then, in a voice equally as hard. "You're not my mother. You're never home."

She cried then in the way she had cried when Elvis died, as if she was losing a part of herself. I watched her, still too mad to want to make up, too drunk to even know how. I had hurt her in a way I hadn't meant to, given voice to the small ache in my heart that had been there ever since she started work, the ache that was the bottle opener for each beer I drank, the match to each joint I smoked. She had deserted me, left me to fend for myself, to figure out when spaghetti was done and how to manoeuvre around my father with the least amount of damage. Even though we lived in the same house, a great distance had spread between us. It felt like being up on the mountain, where you could see people through the trees only fleetingly before they disappeared again. When I was up there with my friends, I knew we'd meet at the summit if we lost each other. I knew where we were heading. With my mother, I wasn't sure.

But she must have known we were heading for a clearing, that sooner or later we'd talk again. And in the days that followed the fight, while we were taking our own paths to that clearing, she sometimes reached out to bridge the distance by doing small and lovely things for me. She'd buy me new hardcover books, pens, and paper, giving me what I needed to navigate my path alone. She always believed I was a writer, and in that way, a part of her nurtured what would turn out to be one of the most important things in my life.

There were times when the distance between us would evaporate. Sunday afternoons, as I sat at the kitchen table writing a seven-hundred-word essay about the Hudson's Bay Company or a poem about my favorite character in *Hamlet,* my mother would put on one of her records, bang the pots and counters with a wooden spoon, and get our dog, Muffin, prancing around her in a crazy excitement that was contagious. We'd chase Muffin around then, my mother and I, her going one way through the living room and me the other way, the dumb and wildly happy dog trapped between us, panting and grinning in the way that only a dog can.

Muffin wasn't the smartest dog. She'd run into glass doors and howl at the couch when she couldn't see her ball. On the afternoon she got hit by a car after chasing our cat right out the back door and onto the street, my mother and I picked her up and carried her to our car without any talking or planning. We moved as if we were one person, gently placing the dog on the back seat and covering her with the blanket she liked sleeping on. We drove to the vet's in silence and stood by Muffin while the vet set her broken leg, taking turns saying good-night to her when we had to leave her there. Each of us had complained at one time or another about the dog, the way she ate anything she could find and then threw it up, the way she needed to go out so often, but we both remarked on how strange it was going home without her, opening the back door without her enthusiastic greeting. The house was quieter without the dog, different. "You don't miss something until it's gone," my mother said then, standing in the middle of the kitchen, her coat unbuttoned but still on, her face lined in a tired way I hadn't noticed before. Though she was referring to Muffin's absence, I got the feeling she was talking about something much bigger, much more important than that. The silence lingered around us like a presence, a haunting, and I felt sad, though I didn't know why.

★ ★ ★

I think now of my mother all those years ago, outside in winter without a coat, in her slippers, her coffee the first thing she could think of grabbing to free me from my predicament, and I love her fiercely. In her own way, with her own music playing in the background, dressed in her navy slacks, her worn sweater, surrounded by her colors and scissors and paste, my mother stood by me the only way she knew how. She coaxed me to the clearing of myself, waited for me there, and then let me go. In the silence that love so often requires, she didn't say a word as she watched me leave her, to grow up as I did.

SO MUCH
HIROMI GOTO

SHE'S BEAUTIFUL IN HER CAT-EYE GLASSES, *her voice*
yasashii. Gentle. Okāsan draws pictures on your paper lunch bag
and she always, always remembers that the bread on your ham
sandwich has to be toasted, mustard only. Sunshine afternoons
when the golden warmth nods, nods you almost sleeping, the soft
pillow of her lap. She smells nice. You could find her in complete
darkness by smell alone. The dark scares you so much you can't
walk to the bathroom by yourself at night. Your mother doesn't
laugh at your fears. She never laughs at you, a child so proud,
you hate it when adults treat you like a child. Adults speak about
being in love. You're in love with your okāsan like you're in a
bathtub of steaming water after you've come in from a morning
of licking icicles, the snow clumping into frozen pellets on your
mitten.

I turn up the song on the kitchen radio. The duet is so dra-
matic it borders on embarrassing, but I still like it. The

man's voice is impossibly deep and the woman joins his low mourning with her forlorn wail. They've stopped feeling love for each other and they're sharing their pain with the world. I know they're just singers, that this isn't real. But they sing very feelingly.

I feel a lot of things, but love's not on the list, romantic, familial, or otherwise. Okāsan bangs around for the "off" switch on the radio. I smirk and she catches me. Jerks the cord out of the socket. She's ragging on me about my attitude. "Why do I have to ask you to do something so many times?" she snaps. "Can't you vacuum the living room without turning it into an issue? It's just one thing I'm asking of you!"

Her eyes. They've shrunk into crazy tiny pits, and her voice gets higher with each word. She's so ugly with her stupid perm. Why does she scorch her hair into crunchy, burn-victim curls? I'll never be like her. Ever.

"How hard is it to help a little around the house?" Her voice cracks as she gets louder and louder. "Why do all my daughters have such bad attitudes—"

The phone rings.

"Hallo," Okāsan breathes all soft and gentle. "*Hai,*" she murmurs, sweet as honey. "*Soo desu. Ho, ho, ho, ho, ho.*" She laughs softly, like a Japanese soap opera lady.

Hypocrite.

I jerk the vacuum cleaner after me like a stubborn dog. My little sisters are in the living room, playing their freaky game. They scratch this tan patch on the carpet next to the TV, where the Fujimotos' kid puked last summer, then dare each other to sniff it. They laugh like maniacs. Weirdos.

"Get outta here," I sneer.

"We're watching TV," they whine.

I glare at them like I'm capable of anything. They scamper to their bedroom and slam the door. I switch on the vacuum and jab the head around in the center of the carpet. Take, my German shepherd, lurches from her closet bed and limps to the kitchen. She can't stand the noise.

"Here!" Okāsan yells over the whirring roar. She stands next to me, pointing. "Over here. Under the couch. The corners, too."

Does she think I don't know how to vacuum?

"Your Uncle Kikuzou and his wife are coming for supper," she shouts. "I'll have to go to Lucky Dollar Store. And with no proper groceries around here…" Okāsan trails off.

So that's why she's having a conniption about cleaning the living room. She's always like this about company. She thinks people will look and gossip. But we don't even have a Japanese community in this dump town we've moved to. There's no one *to* talk, and Uncle Kikuzou's a jerk. Who cares what he thinks?

"Your father will drink," she adds, her voice dropping as I turn off the vacuum. "Then he'll have a fight with your uncle. You tell him not to drink too much. If I tell him, he gets mad." She smiles at me hopefully.

I want to smash the lamps in the room. I am not my father's keeper. And I won't be their intermediary.

"I'm going out tonight," I mutter, pulling on the cord so it sucks back into the body of the vacuum cleaner.

"Where are you going?" Okāsan demands. "You have

to stay and *aisatsu* to your uncle and aunt."

"Don't worry, I'll greet them properly," I snap. "I'm going out after supper. There's a party at Lee's house."

"Will there be drinking?"

"No," I lie. "His parents will be there."

"You have to be home by eleven." Okāsan's lips are pulled tight. "If you're late for church tomorrow, your father will be mad."

The edges of the dream fold into the dark corners of your room. Your heart pounds so hard you're afraid it will burst. You'd rather die than fall asleep again. You cannot say what you dreamt. The only thing left is a terror so keen you know you've dreamt this a hundred times before. Only one thing will save you. Your last courageous act, you fling the blankets off your sweating body and bolt for your parents' bedroom. The thin cotton nightgown turns from hot and sweaty to icy cold. You stumble to a stop. Will you be in trouble for waking them up? The hallway is so dark. What is it? Okāsan calls from the other side. You push the door open and your mother raises her sleepy head. I had a scary dream, you wobble. Okāsan opens her side of the blankets and, heart blooming, you patter over. You snuggle into the pocket she makes with her body. She warms your icy feet. All is well, your Okāsan murmurs as your eyelids grow heavy.

Heavy metal shakes the walls of the party. The house is a few miles out of town, so no one will complain about the noise. Lee's parents are away on a cruise. Beer caps and bottles clutter the floor and chips have been ground into the carpet. I lick the sickly sweet lemonade and vodka on my lips; panty-remover isn't my favorite party beverage. I prefer rye and Coke with lime, but we couldn't find a bootlegger tonight, so we had to make do with what was in Lee's parents' liquor cabinet. A hollow roaring waxes and wanes inside my eardrums, as if I were holding a seashell to my ear.

The couples who are going steady are already long gone, locked into washrooms and bedrooms. As someone switches the music to country and western, the kids who are single start pairing off to make out. I'm left with a few others in the living room. Maybe the night will deteriorate into strip poker.

"Why don't ya make out with Harlan?" Darren teases.

Harlan? I smile weakly, not wanting to insult him. Harlan looks like a milk-fed calf, ready to become veal.

"But she goes to my church!" Harlan protests.

It's too much. Who wants to be a sex reject, undesired even by someone like Harlan? Not that I've had sex yet. Okāsan always says that it should mean something. That sex isn't something you give away to just anyone. She says a lot of shit. But this seems true, somehow. Sure, I made out with my boyfriend last year. But I didn't go all the way. My older sister comes home covered with hickeys. How stupid is that? They're bruises, she tells my parents. Brilliant. An abusive boyfriend is more acceptable than a horny one?

"Are you and Janny lesbians?" Ray jokes. Eyebrows raised.

Heat rises in my face. Janny is my best friend. We go everywhere together. Mutt and Jeff, they call us, because she's tall and I'm short. Janny went home early because she lives beyond the foothills, over an hour away.

"No!" I snap at Ray.

It's time for me to leave, too. The party's gone from bad to worse. How have I become such a reject? Is it because I won't be all giggling-weak? Is it wrong to arm-wrestle with the boys in my class?

I stand outside and bum a cigarette from someone. Fake-inhale so smoke comes out my nostrils. Tar and nicotine coat my tongue, acrid and sour. I spit. Catch a ride back into town.

Light spills through the screen door in the back. I stand beneath the crab apple tree and gaze up at the open kitchen window. I can't hear voices. Uncle Kikuzou and Aunt Mina must have gone home, thank god. There's no yelling, either. Maybe Otōsan's passed out already. The radio's on, and orchestra music trickles out into the warm night air. It seems safe to go inside.

I can't wait to get away from this place. Only three more years and I can start the beginning of the rest of my life.

The screen door screeches.

"Who's that?" Okāsan calls from the living room. "Come in here so I can see you."

I go, but I crouch down next to Take and scratch behind her ears. I don't want Okāsan thinking I'll follow all of her orders. Take's not an affectionate pet, though, and soon she struggles to her feet and clack-clacks to the kitchen. Okāsan's lying on the couch, her cheeks flushed. She's waving an imaginary baton to the classical music. Sounds like Handel.

"Were you drinking?" she asks.

I gauge her mood, then opt for the truth.

"A little."

"Let me see your eyes." She gestures me over.

I roll my eyes but do as she says. I'm not pissed, so I don't have anything to hide.

"You've been smoking!" she admonishes. "You won't be able to quit!"

"I don't inhale," I say.

"Talk with me." Okāsan tugs my hand, all chummy, pats the cushion next to her and smiles.

I roll my eyes again and sink to the couch.

"You're so lucky you have sisters," Okāsan says. "My childhood was very lonely. I didn't have anyone to talk to."

God. The same old song. Hasn't she noticed I haven't exchanged one civil word with my older sister in the past three months?

"Just because you have sisters doesn't mean they're your friends," I mutter sourly.

"Family is family." Okāsan is firm. "No matter what, family will always be there for you."

She actually believes what she's saying. When she and Otōsan scream at each other almost every night. When they resort to blows. Who wants the family to be there for you if all it's about is rage? She's an idiot.

A waltz spills out of the radio. The one-two-three, one-two-three of stringed instruments and brass. The melody is ridiculously happy, and Okāsan leaps to her feet. She throws her arms out wide. "Dance with me!"

Before I can answer she clasps my hand so hard it almost hurts, curves her other arm around my back. She's standing too close, pushing me around in time to the music. My legs are stiff, and I stumble as if I'm falling. Okāsan smiles, like we're having fun. I stare back coldly. Yank my hand out of hers and step away.

"Good-night." I turn and head for the washroom.

"Don't be late for church," Okāsan's tired voice trails after me.

I'm sorry, you bawl. I won't ever do it again. I'm sorry, I'm sorry! you wail. You're so scared and sorry you don't even remember what you did. Because you've been bad enough to deserve yaito. If only you could take it back. The notlisteningbreakingthings-embarrassingtheminfrontofcompany. But it's too late for apologies. Way too late, and your Okāsan strikes a wooden match right in front of your bawling face. The flame is orange and the stink of sulfur fills your nostrils. You can feel the heat against your cheek. You start struggling, twisting to escape, but you're held tightly. She blows out the flame, but the top still glows orange. You're yanked around and the matchstick is ground into the back of your neck. You think you hear sizzling.

You spend the evening in the washroom, using two mirrors to look for the scar. Okāsan doesn't hold grudges. She loves you the next day. You burned me! you accuse. There's a mark! There's nothing there, Okāsan laughs. Besides, in Japan, people pay to have yaito done. They burn medicine on top of the skin to bring out the toxins.

You don't care what they do in Japan. You burned me, you mutter.

Weekdays are hard, but weekends are harder. I had a boyfriend last year, Danny, but he broke up with me because I wouldn't have sex. I thought I loved him, but I still didn't want to do it. Even before we broke up, I lost the neck-lace he gave me somewhere in the grass of our backyard. Maybe it was a sign. Anyway, I've been dateless since. One afternoon this sometimes-friend of mine was flirting with a boy on the phone. She'd met him at the drive-in. She was trying to set me up with the guy's friend, and when she said my name out loud there was a long pause. "It's Japanese!" she explained after a minute. "She's really funny."

Worldwide euphemism for: She's not sexy and beau-tiful, but as long as you're not looking for a "date" date, she's good for a laugh. God. Why not just put a bag over my head and be done with it?

It's Saturday night and I'm in my bedroom with Marty, my stuffed dog. From the radio, a song about sad eyes yanks the strings attached to my heart. Hot tears threaten to drip out. Stupid. Janny, who's considered even more frigid than I am, has a date tonight. My sometimes-friend is grounded, so I'm alone. It's not fair. Life's so unfair.

Okāsan knocks once, then pushes through. I angrily drag my forearm across my eyes. Okāsan sits on the edge of my bed, and I roll over onto the other twin bed to escape any contact. But she shuffles closer, persistent. Looks directly into my face.

"I know you don't get asked out on dates," she begins.

Tears fill my eyes again. Why can't she leave me alone?

"But I know you're special."

Who wants to be *special*? Special means you're a freak or a retard.

"Your father's brought us to this town so we can have a bigger mushroom farm. But the people here have small-town ideas. You're not the same as them. When you leave this place, you will meet other people who will know how special and wonderful you are, and they will love you very much. They will understand you and see you for who you are. There are good things in your future. I believe this with my whole heart."

I spin away from my mother and press my face into the blankets. Her words comfort and mortify all at the same time. I might not be lovable, but my mother loves me. If no one will choose me, my mother will. How reassuring. How pathetic.

I don't care at all about some hypothetical person in the future. I'm me, here, right now. Ugly and unwanted. Okāsan rubs my back for a while, and I'm so lonely I let her.

Tomorrow, I'll have to be extra bitchy so she'll know she's not my friend.

The minister at our church looks like a fish. His cheeks balloon and flap like gills. He's such a terrible public speaker I don't know why he ever chose this occupation. Maybe he was called and he couldn't refuse, like Moses. We rise up to sing, and Otōsan and Okāsan flip through their hymn books while they listen to the opening bars of the song. When they find the corresponding hymn in their books, they sing along in Japanese. The rest of the congregation, of course, sings in English.

Last night's drinks are seeping out of Otōsan's suit. The autumn heat wave doesn't help. Okāsan nudges him with her elbow and he pops a mint into his mouth. Otōsan might be considered handsome in a different time and place, but his eyes are pouchy with lack of sleep. Okāsan's voice is pretty when she sings, but I hate it when she goes all fake-opera. My older sister's up shit creek because she got home after curfew last night. She's grounded for a month, so she'll miss the big party at Rod's place next weekend. As I look over at her, she tugs the bandana she's tied around her neck to hide her latest hickey. She must be roasting in this heat. I snicker with my shoulders so she'll notice. My younger sisters are cloistered in the back room with the other little kids, playing with felt cut-outs of Jesus and his sheep.

After the hymn's over, I slump onto the pew. The minister is mumbling. Drone. Drone. Why do our parents make us come? It seems unchristian to force someone to attend a religious service when they don't believe. I flip through my Bible to Revelation. With all the monsters and satanic creatures, it's almost as good as a Stephen King novel.

At home after church, Okāsan announces that my older sister and I have to pick mushrooms for the rest of the day. My younger sisters have to make boxes.

This is the worst way to be told, without notice or time to prepare. I was going to call up Janny and see if I could go horseback riding at her house. It's Sunday afternoon. Isn't it supposed to be the Lord's day of rest?

"Why didn't you tell us yesterday?" I grit my teeth. "I have plans for this afternoon."

"Your Otōsan went to check the mushrooms this morning," my mother smiles, trying to appease me. "The hot night made them grow faster than usual."

"It's no fair," I whine. "I still have homework. We worked last weekend—"

"Enough!" Okāsan barks. "You don't have to go! You stay home and do what you like!"

I hate it when she does that, the big guilt trip. But it works. Being lazy is worse than being stupid in my family.

"All right! All right!" I hiss, and I stomp out of the kitchen.

Okāsan lets me drive the couple of miles from our house to the farm. The mushrooms are grown inside two huge concrete-block buildings. Thirteen growing rooms are on staggered cycles so that four to six rooms are ready for picking every day of the year. I envy the wheat farmers who spend all winter drinking coffee and gossiping at the gas station diner.

Once I've given up on having fun, mushroom picking's not so bad. The rooms are cool and dark, protected from the glare and blast of the sun. I hold a curved paring knife in my right hand as I pluck mushrooms from the beds of peat moss with my left. When I'm holding three or four, I snick off the root bottoms. The tump-tump-tump-tump of their landing beats rhythmic against the bottom of my metal pail.

We climb higher and higher on the stacked beds until we've picked our way to the top. It's a relief to get there. An accomplishment. My sister's head is just visible; she's picking two rows over. I look around. Okāsan's still at ground level. I cork a root bottom at my sister's head.

Thwack!

"Ow!" she screeches. "Okāsan!"

"Don't waste mushrooms," Okāsan scolds.

"It was only a root," I retort.

"Pick it up after, or it'll rot and make green mold," Okāsan lectures.

My sister gives me the finger. I flip one back. Sigh. Four fifty-three p.m. We won't get a supper break until six. Otōsan's whistling outside the room, and the melody echoes down the long, damp corridor. Sounds like Beethoven.

Thwack!

"Ow!" I yelp. Look indignantly around.

Okāsan, giggling, clambers to the ground.

You're small for a ten-year-old, but you're old enough to clean your own ears if you want. Yet you hold up the bamboo ear-cleaning spoon for Okāsan. She gestures to a spot by the window where the sun slants down all warm and cozy. You lie with your head in her lap. She dips the long-stemmed bamboo spoon into the depths of your ear and scratches gently, gently in the reaches you'll never see. This is something your family does; you don't talk about it with your friends. The scritch-scratching is so exquisite you can barely stand it. You feel so safe. You could stay there forever.

The weekend circles around again. Aside from English class and sports, I could do without school. The weekend breaks the monotony, but then social torture resumes. I want to be like everyone else, and that means being desirable to the opposite sex. It's everywhere all around. See me, love me, adore me. It's just that it's impossible to play the part. Blonde. Big-busted. Simpering.

My older sister is in her room listening to AC/DC. The bass must be pounding the wax out of her ears. I'm going to Rod's party, but she can't. Janny's coming over to curl my hair and put on my makeup. When I do it myself, I end up with kinky cowlicks in my bangs and circles of blush on my cheeks like a Raggedy Ann doll.

As we leave for the party, Okāsan's having drinks with Otōsan in the kitchen. Her face is flushed-happy, and Otōsan hands me a ten-dollar bill.

"Don't drink too much," Okāsan says. Because she can't wink, she blinks both eyes emphatically instead.

Three hours later, I'm shit-faced. Who drove me home? The lawn heaves under me, and the night air's so hot. My eyes are shrinking. My head expanding. Oh Lord. Please. The lights in the house are turned off. I stagger through the back door and try not to let it bang. I stumble to my room, the stairs lurching from side to side. I'm a sailor. A penguin. A pissed teenage girl.

Salt pools in my mouth. I swallow. My room is an oven. I peel my clothes off, drop them where I stand. I slump to the bed nearest me and lie on the rolling surface. The storm tosses my flimsy life raft. I grip the edges of my bed, afraid of drowning. The ceiling spins faster and faster. I'll be lost in the vortex. Desperate, I shut my eyes. Gush of bile and vodka. I roll over and puke in the crack between the twin beds. Ohhh god.

I should clean it up. But I can't move. I'm pinned to my stinking bed. I'm a butterfly. A moth, feeble and hopeless. I will die if I so much as turn my head. My body burns.

A hand strokes my forehead.

I can't bear it. Every sensation is overload. Any sensation will make me throw up again.

"Don't," I croak. I manage to open my eyes and see Okāsan's dark shadow.

I'm in so much trouble.

Okāsan leaves my side silently, then comes back holding something in her hands. I close my eyes. I'm so sick I don't care how mad she is.

Every sound is amplified. A liquid trickling of water almost tips me over the edge again. A wet, warm towel is placed on my shoulder. My skin crawls.

"Don't touch me." I try to push her away, but Okāsan ignores me, wiping the towel gently over my naked shoulders and down my arms, chest, and stomach.

"Get away," I moan. But she's wringing out the towel over the basin again and sliding it down my legs. And I start to notice. The warm water on my skin, so unbearable at first, evaporates in tiny droplets into the night air. The liquid sizzling off my burning skin is like minute pieces of ice crystallizing. A ripple of goose flesh washes over my flaming body. My core temperature drops. The night is bearable. I'm a child again. The child I used to be when I trusted my mother with my world.

Okāsan doesn't say anything at all. She drops the towel into the basin with a tiny splosh. I hear her wiping up the floor, then going back downstairs.

As the last of the moisture rises off my skin, I slip into sleep.

THE SOUND OF DISHES IN THE SINK
TAIEN NG-CHAN

Suburbia

IT HAS ALWAYS BEEN JUST MY MOTHER AND ME. By the time I was ten, I knew how to cook the rice myself, before Mom got home from work. Then she'd make the rest of dinner, maybe soy-sauce chicken or tomatoes and egg, and we would eat. Later, I'd lie in bed, listening to my mother in the kitchen doing the dishes. The clinking of plates and glasses seemed the most comforting sound in the world.

That was in our old place. It was on a street where all the houses looked exactly alike, attached together in a row. We'd lived there for most of my life, but I didn't really have any friends. All the ones I'd grown up with had moved somewhere else and I couldn't seem to make new ones. It was as if I didn't know how. I cried about it once, sobbing until my whole body shook. My mom put her arms around me. "You just have to ask people to be your friends, and they will," she said. I pulled away from her and ran to my room. She had no clue, I realized. I mean, you couldn't simply ask someone to be your friend.

One day when I was thirteen, my mom came home all excited. She had decided to buy us a new house. It was really far away. Our old house was a block away from a mall, and the new one was right by a field. The first time we went to see it, we had to take a bus that went on forever, past where the city ended, until there was nothing but dirt. The houses out there were still being built.

My mom hugged me when we finally saw it. It looked like the skeleton of a house, with all its wooden bones showing. She took a picture of me standing outside it and then asked what color of carpet I wanted in my room. I chose blue.

I decided then that I would be brave and change my life. I would become addicted to *Seventeen* magazine, get contacts, and start wearing makeup. I would be as un-myself as I could. No one would know me at my new school, so this was the perfect opportunity. I was going to be popular.

The first night in our new home, I went to bed in my new, blue-carpeted room with boxes scattered all over the floor. Tomorrow, I'd be taking a school bus for the first time in my life. I lay awake, waiting to hear the sound of dishes clinking in the sink.

My New Friends

I'm in grade eleven now. My mom and I have been living in our new house for over two years, and so many things have changed. Not only the obvious things like where I go to school or church. I can feel myself becoming a different person in a million little ways, but it's not exactly how I planned it.

I've actually managed to make friends at my new school. In fact, I'm even hanging out with the popular kids. This is mostly because of Zinnia, who was my partner in English class when we had to read Shakespeare plays out loud. She's Chinese, too, so we get to laugh together at the stuff our parents do.

Zinnia is my ticket to the in-crowd. Everyone likes her because she's genuinely sweet, and she's pretty, too, with long black hair cut into bangs in the front, and a round face that makes her look like a doll. She's athletic, plays on the school volleyball team, and is everything I'm not. The first time I brought Zinnia home, my mother spent an hour asking her questions like "What are you going to be when you grow up?" I thought Zinnia would never want to come back. But Zinnia smiled and said, "Your mom's cute!" Mom invites her over for dinner all the time now.

Out of all the preppy, well-dressed, in-crowd kids, Zinnia's the only one I can really call my friend. The rest of them are stuck-up and shallow, and they don't much like me, either. But I try to dress and talk like them. My mom is really happy that I seem to be popular. I always come home tired after hanging out with Zinnia's gang, though. It takes so much effort.

Zinnia and I go to the year-end dance together. Before the last dance is over, she finds me and wants to leave. I don't mind. But then she tells me she wants to go meet her boyfriend, K.C., at Edgeworthy Park, where there's a bonfire party. She's convinced Britt and Allison to go, and now she's trying to convince me. I'm the one with the car.

"Come on," she says. "Simon and Jason are going too."

"Why don't you catch a ride with them?" I suggest.

"Puh-leeeeeeze come? You're the one who takes care of me." Zinnia starts making cow's eyes at me and then Britt and Allison start in, too, though I know they don't really care if I come or not.

"Okay, but I have to leave by midnight," I finally tell Zinnia. She hugs me, drags me out to the parking lot. A gang of people is there already, waiting for us.

Eleven people, including me, pile into the car. The back seat is crammed full and they're all yelling out the window. I weave in and out of the traffic, taking the turnoff into the park as fast as I can, to be a daredevil. Everyone screams as they crash into one another. I pull into the parking lot and turn off the headlights.

Edgeworthy Park is full of strange, gray shadows. I feel like remaining on the edge of things, shadowlike myself, so I can watch people as they weave intricate lines among themselves, begin the rituals of pairing off. I feel too tired to keep up this charade of being cool, and I keep thinking that I should be getting home. K.C. spots us from the small crowd around the fire, and Zinnia goes off with him. I don't know what else to do, so I follow Britt and Allison, but soon they've given me the slip. My heart feels like a flat tire. I hang out by the car until almost midnight, and just when I've made up my mind to leave, Zinnia shows up with the others. So I drive them home.

This same scenario happens over and over, with me tagging along like a lost puppy, until one day I stop making the effort. That's how I remember it, but maybe it was so gradual a change that I didn't even notice. It's like I woke up one day and found myself a completely different person, someone who didn't bother fitting in. I like being this person better. I begin to wear my difference on the outside, small things at first, like going to school in old ripped jeans when everyone else has new ones. Being different gives me something to claim as my own.

My New Church

When Mom and I moved to our new house, we found a new church to go to as well. Mom discovered a Chinese Presbyterian congregation, and right away she made friends there. Pastor Chang is such a nice man, she says, and so smart. She's started to go to his Wednesday night Bible Study classes, and Friday night Prayer Group as well.

We didn't always go to church. But a girl in my grade-five class, who was a Jehovah's Witness, would tell me stories at recess about how the people who weren't saved were going to hell. I'd run home crying. "What's wrong?" my mother would ask me, and all I could say between sobs was "You're going to hell … waaaahhh!"

The other kids in my old neighborhood all went to a Baptist church. Every Friday night, they had Youth Group, where they did fun things like rollerskating and going on hayrides. Next thing you know, I was praying and Bible-studying with the best of them. Finally, I convinced my mother to come along, too. She found the Lord in a way I never did, and she's been going to church ever since.

One Sunday morning, Mom comes into my room, still in her housecoat, her short, permed hair a bit frizzy. "Get up!" she says. "Time to go to church!"

"Oooooh, just a few more minutes," I moan, rolling over.

"Okay," she says, leaving me curled up under the covers.

I lie there for a while, and I think about getting up. I know it would make Mom happy if I went with her.

Fifteen minutes go by, then she knocks on my door. "Get up!"

I don't get up.

Half an hour later she comes into my room, her makeup nicely done and her hair in neat curls. She's carrying her best handbag and already has her long black coat on.

"I'm going now," she says. "You don't want to come today?"

"I'm sooo tired," I groan.

"What time did you get in last night?"

"Just after midnight."

"Okay. But you'll come next week? Pastor Chang keeps asking about you."

"Yeah, I promise." I wait to hear the sound of the front door closing. Then I get up and turn on the TV.

No one at my new school goes to church, and in the last few months, I've only gone a couple of times. I do like the hymn-singing. But some of the things Pastor Chang says make no sense to me. Sometimes he even makes me mad. *Rock and roll is bad,* he'll say, and I can tell he doesn't know anything about being young. *Abortion is wrong, killing babies is wrong,* he'll say. I don't know what to think about that.

Maybe it *is* wrong, but what if I got pregnant? Most of the time at church, though, I'm simply bored. Wade and I agree that boredom is pretty much the worst state to be in.

That's something else that's new. Wade.

My New Boyfriend

I call Wade my boyfriend, but I'm not sure that's entirely correct. The question really isn't there between us. When I first met him, he was hanging out with Zinnia's crowd, but he stood apart from them with his vampire-pale skin and black-dyed hair and horn-rimmed glasses hanging crooked off the end of his sharp nose. His teeth are a bit crooked, too. He transferred from a school that has the reputation of being tough, and he's a year older than we are, so that makes him cool. I see him hanging out with the heads, too, on the compound where they all smoke.

The first time Wade and I hung out, we went for dinner and then walked around for a while. I wasn't thinking it was a date, because everyone knows he used to go out with Carolyn Murray. She's a model, so I assumed that's the kind of girl he liked. But before I got into my car, he said, "I'm always kind of awkward about this," then bent down, surprising me by lightly brushing his lips against mine. We still kiss sometimes, but it's never in a deep, making-out way. Sometimes we hold hands, too. But mostly, we talk.

Wade and I talk about everything, about school and religion (*opium of the people!*) and all the wars being fought in the world over God. We agree that people in general are mostly pretty stupid. Wade, who reads more than anyone

I know, starts lending me books like George Orwell's *Down and Out in Paris and London* and Jack Kerouac's *On the Road*. Sometimes we show each other our poetry. With him, I feel like what I think and do might actually matter. Wade's a vegetarian, and I start eating less meat. I also resolve never to go back to church.

The New Me

I come home one day and chop my hair off really short with my mom's sewing scissors. Then comes hours with Miss Clairol and Super Blondissima and even bleach from the laundry room. My hair is very black and thick, so it isn't easy to get it blonde. It only gets to an ugly shade of orange before I dye it a neon pink. "Whoa," Zinnia says when she sees me. "You look so tough!" Mom freaks out on me, but not as much as she does on the day I come home with a nose ring. I've never heard her yell as much as she does then.

She says things like, *You were such a pretty girl. Why you want to look so ugly for? Who taught you that?*

I say things like, *This is who I am! You don't understand me at all! You only love me if I look the way you want me to look!*

This fighting is new, and it shocks me sometimes. But it's exciting, too. I feel as if I'm playing a role, watching myself on TV. I never know what I'm going to do next.

One Saturday, my mom decides to takes me shopping. At first, I want to go. I want to get some new T-shirts. But once we're standing in an aisle of girls' clothing, it's all cutesy and pastel. Hasn't my mom noticed I wear only black now?

"How about this?" she says to me in Chinese. She holds up a preppy button-down shirt. It's pink.

"I don't like anything here," I say testily.

"Why? This is nice! How about a skirt?" She holds up a pale-blue skirt, with pleats.

"Noooooo! Let's just go."

"What's wrong? I wanted to buy you some good clothes," she says.

"What do you mean, good? Don't you like what I have on?" Lately, I've taken to wearing army boots and ripped tights.

"It's old!" My mother wrinkles her nose. "And how come you buy secondhand? You always used to dress so pretty!"

"So now you think I'm ugly. Well, you can GO TO HELL, okay?"

I have never, ever said this to my mom. But there I am, in the middle of a department store, yelling it at her, and then stalking away furiously. I leave her standing there bewildered, and take the bus over to Zinnia's house. I am thinking I will never go back home.

"Are you going to run away?" Zinnia asks.

"Maybe," I say. But I hang around until evening, and then I call my mom. I'm scared that she'll be really mad at me, but she isn't.

"Come home," she says.

So I do.

In the morning, my mom wakes me up with a hug and says, "Breakfast is ready!" I get up to have toast and tea with her. Every day, we start over.

Prayer Group

Mom's different since she started going to church so much. She prays every night now, and says a long grace before meals. She keeps asking me to come with her to Prayer Group and Bible Study. It would mean a lot to her, so sometimes I think about going. But that would undo all this work of stopping. Then she would never quit nagging me to go to church.

Tonight my mom's Prayer Group is meeting at our house. She wants me to be there, and I keep saying no. Zinnia wants me to go with her to meet K.C. and his friends tonight at the Warehouse, a bar downtown. We're underage, not yet seventeen, but she thinks she can swing this one. She's got fake ID for herself and her sister's old ID for me, even though her sister is twenty-five. We make jokes about how the white-boy bouncers at the club won't be able to tell the difference anyway.

K.C. is an asshole and a two-timing jerk. Zinnia's so beautiful, and everyone likes her, yet she's going out with this guy who's twelve years older than she is. Why can't he find someone his own age? K.C.'s a mechanic, and always has the smell of grease on him. He's got a big moustache and big arms, and thinks everything's a big joke. I'd like to give him a good punch, but it probably wouldn't do much good unless I used a crowbar. I've told Zinnia what I think of him, and she agrees, but maybe she's in love with his muscles. She's broken up with him before, but she always goes back.

After dinner, I head out the door. "I'm going over to Zinnia's!" I call out to my mom.

"Bring her over tonight!" she calls back. "Prayer Group starts at eight o'clock!"

"I told you, I'm going out!"

She comes out of the kitchen, where she's been making snacks, and shakes her head at me. "Would it be so hard to stay home one night? You never do anything with me anymore."

Uh-oh, the guilt trip. My mom is amazing at this.

"Always with your friends," she continues. "And always coming home late. No time for your mother!"

"Alright, already! I'll be home at eight!"

But she doesn't know when to stop. "You know, I talked to Pastor Chang about you. He says you are only growing up. But the way you act! Who taught you such things? I don't know what to do with you!"

That's the last straw. "Why can't you just leave me alone?" I scream at her. "I HATE YOU!" I run out of the house, slamming the front door.

When I get to Zinnia's, her mother is pouring a bottle of booze into the sink and her father is shouting from the next room.

"I can't stay too long," I say. "I have to be back for my mom's stupid prayer meeting."

"But you're coming tonight, right? You promised."

"Don't worry, I'll be there."

We go around to the backyard where they have rabbits in a pen. Zinnia lets me hold one. It's a baby, so small it fits in my hand. It kicks with its hind legs against my thumb, just a little, and then lets me stroke its tiny belly.

The prayer meeting has started by the time I get home.

I sit in the corner, mind-numbingly bored. When my mother asks everyone to pray for me, I scowl at her, and she throws me dirty looks across the room.

After the group finally leaves, I get into bed with my clothes still on. I lie there in the dark, waiting until all the lights have gone out and I can hear my mother lightly snoring. Then I get up, and sneak out the front door.

The fake IDs work and we get past the bouncers. Inside the Warehouse we see K.C. immediately, standing by the bar. Zinnia sits on his lap the entire night, so I go onto the dance floor by myself, and dance. It feels good not to think about anything.

Just before the Warehouse is about to close, K.C. and Zinnia have a big fight in the parking lot. I drag her away from him, and drive her home. She fumes about him all the way there. When I drop her off, she gives me a hug good-bye. And then she says, almost as an afterthought, that her period is late. She laughs in mock horror, like, *Oh no, here we go again!* because she's often late. She gets out of the car, and I watch her open her front door carefully, then disappear into the dark house.

I head home, driving fast and north on Fourteenth Street, the city lights spread out below like brown and white sugar granules spilled onto a dark tablecloth.

The Talk

One day my mom decides it's time to have a Talk. I bet Pastor Chang has put her up to it.

"Don't you believe in God?" she begins. "You know, if you pray to him, he will answer you."

I shake my head. Wade and I have talked a lot about how God is just a way for the Church to tell us what to do. I'm not sure how I really feel, though. I want to believe there is someone looking out for me, but in the end it seems too simple, too full of *whys*. "I don't know," I tell my mom. I can see this genuinely distresses her, so I pull back.

"Okay, maybe I believe in *a* God," I tell her. "But maybe not *your* God."

She furrows her brow, like she doesn't get it. "What do you mean?"

"I don't believe everything the Bible says. Like, did you know there's a part that says a woman shouldn't speak in church? It says all sorts of things about women in there."

My mom doesn't push me on this, but it doesn't matter. I'm on a roll. I start spouting off about how angry the Church makes me and how stupid it is and how I never want to go back.

Suddenly, she says, "Okay!" She's angrier than I've seen her in some time. "You don't have to say those things! Always *stupid this, stupid that*. Yelling all the time. I have feelings too!" She gets up and walks out of the room. We don't speak for the rest of the day.

Tests

I've never seen anyone cry the way Zinnia is crying. Her whole body is shaking in great heaves. I want to make it okay, but there's nothing I can say to make that happen.

"What am I going to do? What I am going to do?" she says, over and over. I do the only thing I can think of. I take her to the free clinic downtown. No one there asks for your parents' medicare number, and they don't ask stupid questions, either. I've already been to the clinic once to get the Pill. Wade and I aren't sleeping together—not even close—but I wanted to have them, just in case.

The waiting room has magazines from ten years ago, old *Seventeen*s and *Flare*s. The girls in them look so strange. Zinnia and I wait all afternoon, watching a rectangle of sun move over the receptionist's desk and shift across the floor. Finally, a nurse comes along and ushers us into her office to tell us that Zinnia's pregnancy test is positive. Zinnia begins to cry. The nurse looks at me, looks away. I hug Zinnia and then I drive her home.

When we get to her house, Zinnia refuses to get out of the car. "My dad's going to kill me," she says. She sits there for a long time, twisting her necklace into knots around her fingers.

"Do you want to go somewhere?" I ask her.

"I don't have anywhere *to* go."

"Let's walk."

We head down to the river and walk for hours, until long after dark. Finally, Zinnia says, "I'd better go home now." I walk her back and then drive home.

Mom's been waiting up for me. I can tell by the flickering blue lights in the living-room window. "Hi, Mom!" I call as I close the front door and lean down to take off my shoes.

"Hi," she calls back. "I was just going to bed."

She's watching TV in her nightgown. I take off my coat and sit down beside her on the couch.

"Did you have fun with your friends tonight?" she asks.

I shrug. My bones feel heavy and achy-tired, but I don't want to go to sleep yet. I lean my head on her shoulder and we watch TV for a while, some old movie in black and white.

I've noticed before that when my mom watches television, she doesn't really pay attention. She glances at the images on the screen, and sometimes she makes comments on the actors and actresses—"Oh, that's Katherine Hepburn" or "Ah, Kirk Douglas." But mostly she stares off slightly to the side of the screen, caught up in her own thoughts. She's doing that now. I never ask what she's thinking.

After a while, she sniffs at my hair and says "Aiyaaah, have you been smoking?"

I *had* been bumming cigarettes the night before, and I haven't washed my hair yet. But of course I don't tell her that. I say it's because Zinnia and I sat in the smoking section of a restaurant. She's satisfied with this. She goes back to watching the TV and the space next to it.

Choices

Within three days, the rumor has gotten around school about Zinnia. I haven't told anyone except Wade, and I know he wouldn't say anything. I bet Zinnia told Britt or Allison. She's terrified that her parents will find out, because her father will kick her out of the house. "K.C. doesn't have any money," Zinnia tells me. She says this in a whisper.

"I bet he's got *some* money," I say. "He's got a job, hasn't he?"

"He says he's got a lot of bills to pay." Zinnia starts crying again, but she no longer sobs out loud. Instead, tears run fast and smooth down her face, silently. "I don't know what to do," she says. Neither do I.

That night after dinner, I'm lying on the couch watching TV. Nothing's on, so I flip through channels endlessly. I can hear my mother doing the dishes in the kitchen, and for some reason, it makes me a bit sad. I go and stand next to her, putting my head on her shoulder.

"Hello," she says.

"Hi, Mom," I say back. Then, without thinking, I start telling her everything. All about Zinnia and how she's pregnant and wants an abortion but her jerk of a boyfriend won't give her any money, won't take responsibility. How she's going to get kicked out.

"Zinnia can put the baby up for adoption," my mother says. "We'll help her."

"You're not listening," I say. "Where is she going to *have* the baby? Where will she live?"

"I'm sure her parents won't make her leave."

"Yes, they will. They kicked her sister out because they didn't like her boyfriend. Maybe she should come live with us."

Mom turns off the taps and peels off her rubber gloves. "You have a good heart," she says. She wipes her eyes with the back of her hand.

Later that night, I call Zinnia and ask her to come over. When she arrives, my mom takes her into the kitchen. They are in there for a long time.

I have the TV on in the living room. From time to

time, I mute the sound, but I can't hear them talking.

"What did she say?" I ask Zinnia when she comes out.

"She asked me what I wanted to do, and I told her I wanted an abortion."

"She's against abortion." I should know this; I've heard it often enough at church.

"Well, she didn't say that. She said I should think hard about it."

"Really?"

"Yeah. Then she gave me this." Zinnia opens a white envelope to show a stack of twenty dollar bills nestled inside. "It's three hundred dollars. I'll pay her back when I can."

It takes me a few moments to understand, and I'm still sorting it out as I drive Zinnia home. "You're so lucky," she says to me.

When I get home again, Mom's in the kitchen, listening to the kettle beginning to boil. "Do you want a cup of tea?" she asks me.

"Okay," I say. "I'll make it."

I pour boiling water into the teapot, Mom gets the milk and sugar out, and we sit down at our kitchen table together.

WHAT YOU DON'T KNOW

GAYLA REID

I.

I'M SIXTEEN WHEN MY MOTHER has to hurry down to the city. My grandmother has had a stroke.

My father's busy at work; my brother's away on a summer job. School's over for the year, and in the evening the heat stays with us. I sit in the breezeway to read. We call it the breezeway, but it's really a long, screened-in back veranda, with tables and chairs, and a huge old sofa. There are bushes all around the veranda—buddleias, they're called, or butterfly bushes. The buddleias have sturdy flowers in shades of lavender, violet, and white. My mother likes the violet ones best.

One evening, through the buddleias, I glimpse a young man vaulting over the fence from the yard behind ours. He crosses our back garden (*as if he owned the place,* I think) and walks to the screen door.

"Knock, knock," he says, looking right at me. "Anyone home?"

He opens the screen door, comes in, sits at the table on the veranda as if expecting something.

He's on leave from the navy, he says. Staying with his aunt for one week. Mick—that's his name, Mick. His aunt lives in the messy house behind ours. This is an inland town; we know nothing about the navy.

"You can call me Popeye," he says, "but I wouldn't advise it."

I go into the kitchen to fetch him a soft drink. He studies me as I open the bottle, pour the contents into a glass. He's watching so closely I feel as if I'm doing all this in a slowed-down movie.

"Where is everyone?" he asks. I tell him that Dad's at the paper, which has gone on night shift; my brother's working for the summer down at the coast. My mother had to go to the city because my grandmother's been taken seriously ill. I enjoy using the phrase "taken seriously ill."

I'm not close to my grandmother. When we visit she looks at me, does that tedious how-you've-grown, and says, *You look so much like your father.* Later she complains that my father could be working on a metropolitan daily, but oh no, he'd rather bury himself in the town where he grew up.

"Just you then." The young man runs a finger along the glass, which is sweating in the heat.

"Most of the time."

He's wearing a top with no sleeves. His arms are short and thick, full of muscle.

"What do you do in the navy?" I ask.

"As little as possible," he says. I imagine him tying big heavy ropes at a wharf.

On the upper part of his left arm he has a tattoo of a heart. "Got it done in Cairo," he boasts. The heart has a silly scroll over it with the word "Mother." When he flexes, the heart moves as if it's beating.

"Cairo," I say, jumping up. "My parents went to Egypt for their honeymoon." I go into the front room and take the picture from the piano. My mother is on a camel, with the Pyramids in the background.

"That's my mother," I say. Not everybody's mother has seen the Pyramids.

"Is it now?" he says.

Abruptly, he stands up. Moves to the door. Stands, swinging the screen back and forth, making it creak.

"See ya," he says. And is gone.

2.

A few hours later it seems as if perhaps Mick's visit hadn't happened at all. But there is the glass, the empty soft drink bottle. Proof.

I wander into my parents' bedroom. I study myself in the full-length mirror. The last time my mother had to leave in a hurry, I was only three years old. That's my earliest memory of her. She was crying and bundling clothes into a suitcase, not bothering to fold them properly. Before she even had time to brush her hair, the taxi arrived. It was winter, and the wind pulled at her coat.

I lean close to the mirror to check my chin for pimples. I keep thinking about Mick's arms. And how he'd glanced at the picture of my mother, bored out of his mind.

That's my mother. Is it now?

The other time my mother had to rush down to the city, it was because her father had died all of a sudden. That's a cliché, my mother has told me. You should never say things happen *all of a sudden*.

All of a sudden Mick came over the fence. All of a sudden he was gone.

As I sit down at my mother's dressing table, I smell her powder. Not the powder in her compact; she's taken that with her. This powder is soft and pink, in an elaborate round cardboard box with the big, fluffy pom-pom thing she uses to put it on, after her bath.

When I was little, I used to sit on the bed and watch as she got ready to go out. I would wait for the soft sound her green silk dress made as it slid down her body. She'd smooth the dress, then stand with her back to the full-length mirror and look over her shoulder, checking.

The mirror, which is an antique, swings on a wooden frame. At its base is a long, wide drawer. My mother keeps her nightdresses in there. When she left for the city that first time, I crawled into the drawer at the base of the mirror. It had her smell in it, freshly ironed. I closed my eyes. I lay in the enormous hollow that was my mother, gone.

Of course, I can't fit into the drawer anymore. I stand with my back to the mirror, then I look over my shoulder. Quickly, trying to surprise myself.

What does Mick see when he looks at me?

3.

I can tell my mother almost everything, but she wouldn't want to know about Mick. Just as well she's down in the city. She phoned my father on the weekend and said she wasn't sure when she'd be back.

My mother, you understand, is not like the others. "No," she'll tell the other mothers, firmly pushing away invitations, "I never did learn to play cards. You could say I never developed the knack." (I can see them thinking, *Stuck up. Should go back to the city where she belongs.*)

"Card-playing," my mother tells me, "is the pastime of idle country women. I wouldn't want you growing up like that." Instead, we lie on my bed and read books aloud to one another. Or we lie on her big bed, each of us reading in silence.

Unlike the others, my mother has a job. She works with my

father on the newspaper. "I don't know what they find to do with themselves all day long," she'd say, of the stay-at-home mothers. "No wonder they're reduced to sticking bits of fruit in Jell-O."

Not that all the stay-at-home mothers were like that. The woman in the house at the back would slouch around in her slippers all day long, smoking one cigarette after another. She'd open her front door, bang on it with a wooden spoon, and yell into the street, "Youze kids get in here right away." These weren't little kids she was yelling at; they were adolescents. My mother said it was no wonder they'd all bolted as soon as they were old enough.

The woman in the house at the back is Mick's aunt.

When I was little there was a huge fuss about the greyhound dogs at her place. The greyhounds were chained up, which was bad enough to start with. But they'd get away, come flying into our backyard, then over our front fence, and off. Before the buddleias grew around our breezeway at the back, we looked right into the dogs' yard. It was why my mother had planted the bushes.

"Those greyhounds," my mother would say, starting in. "(A) That woman shouldn't keep them in the town. (B) She shouldn't have them chained up. (C) If she is going to have them, they need muzzles when they're out walking."

When my mother said that, I felt scared for Smokey, my kitten. (I knew what greyhounds did when they saw a cat. They thought it was a rabbit.) But I also felt guilty, because I was attracted to the dogs. They had soft brown eyes and sweet expressions. Shy, but keen. When Mick's aunt took the four of them walking early in the morning, their slim heads darted about, getting a good look, smelling everything.

One day the greyhounds came over the fence and went straight for Smokey. My parents had gone to work already, so my brother and I—late for school—had to phone them. My mother jumped in the car and drove home right away. Smokey was beside the veranda, leaning against it. His nose had been torn off. I could see his pink tongue, reaching up into his head. I lay on the ground beside him, saying his name over and over, and trying to pet him. But he didn't want it.

My mother took Smokey away. Then she went round to Mick's aunt's place. When my mother's really mad, her voice becomes low and she starts enunciating very slowly and clearly, as if she's talking to someone who needs to read lips. Her face turns red, then pale, and the muscles in her nose tighten up.

"Breathing fire and brimstone," my brother said. I wasn't sure what exactly brimstone was.

After she'd been to Mick's aunt's, my mother phoned the mayor's office. More precise enunciation.

By the end of the week, the dogs were shut up in a wire enclosure. When the dogs went out for their walks they wore muzzles. My mother said, "Thank heavens for that," and made a little speech at the family supper table about people acting responsibly.

She thought she'd won.

What she didn't know was this: when my parents left for work, Mick's aunt opened the dog run and let the greyhounds free. Their muzzles lay in the grass like instruments from warfare long ago.

Should we tell her? Get her all riled up again? My brother and I discussed it. "What she doesn't know," my brother said, "won't hurt her."

I hated those dogs for having killed Smokey. They loped about, enjoying themselves as if nothing had even happened. The trouble was, part of me still liked them.

4.

My mother calls me her lovely girl and thinks I'm destined for great things. That's what she says to my father: *I do believe my lovely girl is destined for great things.* I tell her I wish she wouldn't. "But I want such things for you," my mother insists. "You," she says, "you will go on and out and up. I can feel it in my bones." If you have a mother who says such things, who even thinks them, you know what a weight that can be.

I came home from kindergarten one day, sat down at the piano, and played "Twinkle, Twinkle Little Star" right through by ear. My mother cried out in triumph. From then on we both played whatever I was learning, with me showing off on the hard bits. We were fooling around with the three shorts and a long at the beginning of Beethoven's Fifth, da–da–da—DAH, and my mother said, "People asked Beethoven what it meant, and he told them it was fate, knocking at the door."

"Youze get in here right away!" I replied. We giggled like crazy.

My mother is convinced I'll grow up to become a concert pianist. Either that or a brain surgeon, says my brother, and punches me in the arm. A concert pianist is what she might have been herself, way back when. If she hadn't fallen for my father. *I really* fell *for your father,* she says, and she laughs as if life had played some incredible joke on her.

For town concerts, my mother puts on her green silk dress and plays the piano. She starts off with something difficult and ambitiously gallopy. At first the audience is bored—they're waiting for the clatter-clatter of the tap dancers. But then she goes to work on them. She begins to play sentimental Irish tunes with such concentration you think you're hearing them for the first time. By the end of the "Danny Boy" encore the audience is on the edge of their seats for the silences in between the notes.

My mother says we should express our feelings, and not be like everyone else in Sleepy Hollow. That's what she calls our town, Sleepy Hollow.

She wants me to tell her everything. Like about my first

real boyfriend, this guy called Raymond Castelli. I'd known Ray Castelli forever (his parents work with my parents). When I started high school, the sight of Ray's back began to make my knees go limp. I didn't exactly rush to tell my mother about this, but she guessed.

The times we really talked about Ray were when he stopped being interested. I'd tell her what I said, what he said, and she'd listen to it all, not interrupting, but considering. Depending on what she thought I needed to hear, she'd say everything would come out all right with Ray, or that it was inevitable I'd find someone new and better, someone who appreciated me more.

I could see right through all this, but it was good to hear. She was on my side, forever.

I will never tell my mother about Mick. Can you imagine? She'd go marching round to the house behind, enunciating clearly and breathing brimstone.

Mind you, I wouldn't mind talking to her about a few things. Mick's started coming over every evening. At the end of each visit, he announces, as if he were a general sending his troops on a top-secret mission, "Gentlemen, time to synchronize watches." We both pretend to look at our watches, and he says, "Next rendezvous, nineteen hundred hours."

I sensed right away that this was something he'd picked up (from another sailor, probably); it felt secondhand. But his face went pink and I realized it was a bit of magic he really wanted. If I could tell my mother all this, she'd be terribly interested. I could ask, How come this joke feels borrowed but at the same time, genuine? We'd puzzle about it, talk it over, examine it this way and that.

5.

Mick's at the screen door again. He's been playing tennis all afternoon.

"Smells as if the last set was in the pub."

"Very funny, young lady." He sits down, full of expectation. I bring him a cold drink.

"Want to go for a drive?" he suggests. "We could get some Chinese food."

"Didn't notice you had a car," I say, to give myself time.

"It's my aunt's."

"Where is your aunt?"

"Sleeping." It could be true, I think; she's old.

I have an image of me and him, sitting in the Chinese restaurant, facing one another across the red plastic table-cloth. By the time we've finished the sweet and sour soup, the whole town will know.

He sees me wavering.

"I can pick it up," he says. "The Chinese food. We can go for a drive and eat it." He laughs as if he's cracked a joke, but maybe he's just nervous.

And this is what's so weird: I don't want to go with him, but I hear myself agreeing.

The idea of Chinese food is immediately abandoned. We simply jump the back fence, run into the garage. Mick starts the car, and I slide down in the front passenger seat until we're out of town.

It comes so naturally, you'd think I've been doing this all my life.

He doesn't mind my sliding down. "Bunch of old busy-bodies," he says, gesturing with his hand to the town in general. I could go along with that. He lights a cigarette, offers me a drag.

"No thanks."

"No thanks," he says, pretending to be imitating my voice, only making it sound high and prissy-missy. I begin to wish I hadn't come. I fiddle with the window. Thank goodness he's taken a back road. Not much chance of anyone seeing us.

He finds a sandy spot by the river—nobody around. He stands on the rocks at the river's edge, skipping stones. Once, twice, three times, four. "Pretty fancy," I say.

"Do you like it here?" he asks. "Not the river, the town."

"I've lived here all my life."

He gives a short laugh. "Well then," he says, "you'd better like it, hadn't you?"

"My father's been all around the world and he says this is the best place to bring up a family."

"I'm sure it is, sweetheart," he replies, bored. He'd been all around the world himself. Or at least to Cairo. (Maybe.)

He sits beside me, takes my left arm. Very deliberately, with pressure, he runs his finger across my hand, up the inside of my arm to my elbow. He stops, then makes small circles with his finger. All the time he's pretending to be watching his finger, but really he's checking my face. He moves his finger farther up. I'm having trouble breathing. He can tell.

He takes off his top, walks into the water with only his jeans on. When I refuse to join him, he calls out, "Stuck-up lot, aren't you?" Turns his back on me, dog-paddles across to the far shore. I remember my mother saying that sailors never know how to swim. Or is that fishermen?

He dog-paddles back, wades out of the water, and comes to stand in front of me in his dripping jeans. I won't look up but I can feel him, above me.

Now we take the car out each evening. Mick waits until nineteen hundred hours, and then he vaults over the back fence, comes into the breezeway. Sits at the table, with me serving him a soft drink and him smoking smelly roll-your-owns. (Good job my father smokes a pipe; my mother claims he's killed all sense of smell sucking on that thing. And I'm careful to empty Mick's ashtray.) When it's dark, Mick goes back, takes the car, and we drive — with me crouched out of sight — until we're in the countryside. It seems unlikely that his aunt goes to bed at dusk every single night, but I don't ask. By the time my father gets off night shift at the paper, I'm back home in bed.

When we reach the river, Mick kisses me. Messes with the hair at the back of my neck. Each time we do a bit more. "Oh baby," he says. Part of me is dizzy, like I'm almost passing out. Part of me is thinking, cut the "oh *baby,*" it's ridiculous.

One night we drive farther than before. After we go to the river he takes us up to a lookout on a mountaintop way behind town. Turns off the engine. Already there are summer fires in the mountains, and I can smell a thin ribbon of smoke. We sit in the dark. He points out stars and claims he's learned celestial navigation.

As soon as he switches off the engine, I think, this is *it.* And, *no.*

He begins telling me how he'd been counting the hours.

I push him away. And again.

Finally, in cold anger, he starts for home. Going down the steep mountain road, he puts the car in neutral. The windows are open and the smell of smoke and dry grass rushes into the car, which picks up more and more speed as it takes the bends. In silence, we fly down the mountainside.

He doesn't switch the engine on until we're at the bottom.

We drive sedately back into town, him staring straight ahead and me in my hideout on the floor. After he parks in the garage, he looks at me and says, "Think what you like, we're not through yet. Not by a long shot."

And the problem is, I love it. The danger, the dark, his demands, my own power in pushing him away. All of that.

When he leaves we don't synchronize watches; he doesn't even suggest it.

6.

Saturday. I want him to come; I don't want him to come. I wait all day. I tell myself, He won't come today, he can't, my father's at home. So when Mick does come vaulting over the fence, I'm taken by surprise.

He looks up into the breezeway and there's my father, lounging on the sofa, reading the weekend papers.

Mick's quick. I can see it on his face: *Go back or not?* He decides to bluff it out. "Shortcut," he says, to my father. I'm right there in the breezeway, sitting at the table. He doesn't look at me.

"That's okay," says my father, and smiles at him in a vague way.

So Mick keeps right on going, out our front gate. I hear the click of the latch.

Tomorrow my mother comes home.

★ ★ ★

On Sunday morning, very early, I hear a taxi honk its horn outside his house. I know what's going on. He's giving his aunt one of those let's-get-this-over-with hugs, then he's climbing into the taxi.

He's gone.

We're not through yet. Not by a long shot.

I lie on my bed. In a waking dream the image floats up of my mother, years ago: her wet face, her untidy suitcase, the taxi arriving too soon. That night when I was three years old and my mother had to go to the city, life went up an octave. At the time I hadn't known about octaves, of course, but I'd sensed that the air was higher, sharper.

That's how it is with Mick. He isn't my boyfriend; that's for sure. I don't know what he is.

My father and I meet the Sunday afternoon train. I watch my mother step down from the train, grin and wave, walk towards us.

I know exactly what she'd think of Mick, if she knew. And I know she'd expect me to think that, too.

My father kisses and hugs her. Then she hugs me. "My lovely girl," she says.

"Oh, Jim," she says, addressing my father, "whatever would I do without the two of you." "Three," she adds, remembering my brother. She walks between us to the car, an arm around each of us. "She's hanging in there," she tells my father, referring to my grandmother.

"So," says my mother, settling into the front passenger seat. "What's been going on around here?"

"Big news," he says, making a joke. "The woman behind us has her nephew staying."

"He's in the navy," I say. It just jumps out. A small pause in the front seat.

"My, that's exciting," my mother says, sarcastic.

"He came over the fence yesterday evening," Dad says. "I think he's taken to using our yard as a shortcut."

"Now that's what I'd call a wild Saturday night in Sleepy Hollow," she says.

★ ★ ★

My mother's lying in the bath, with lots of bubble bath—green apple, her favorite. It doesn't bubble up the way it does in movies. This is one of our oldest rituals: I sit on the bathroom chair, in the warm steamy atmosphere, and we talk. When I was little I'd climb in behind her and wash her back. My mother says we're like the Romans. They did a lot of socializing at their baths.

I can't tell her about Mick. So what am I going to say? Say I've been playing a lot of tennis, and going swimming? It's not as though she'll check up on me; she isn't like that.

The trouble is, when she looks at me, her face is full of confidence. In us, in the way we share things. Mick has confidence too, but of such a different kind.

Maybe I could tell her a little. Leave out all the car bits, definitely. I could mention he came over and we talked. He told me he's in the navy; he's been to Cairo. (Forget the tattoo.) He's learned celestial navigation, he knows how to steer by the stars. She'd like the idea of celestial navigation; she'd go for that.

I've been asking her tons of questions, to keep her mind on Grandmother and not on me. She's got her heavy voice on, the one she uses when she feels everything fits together and makes sense, but in a sad way. "It's a big challenge," she tells me, "to acknowledge you may be facing your end."

She jiggles the tap with a foot. Her toenails are their bright tulip red. My grandmother may be facing her end, but my mother's found time to paint her nails.

She sighs, lies back, closes her eyes, sticks her little fingers in her ears, and submerges her head. Her hair spreads out, floats. I study her face, beneath the water. *We're not through yet, not by a long shot.*

When she surfaces, gasping for breath, she says, "Your turn, my lovely girl. What I really want to know is, what's been happening with you?"

ABOUT THE AUTHORS

HIROMI GOTO is the author of the award-winning novels *The Kappa Child* and *Chorus of Mushrooms*. Her first children's fantasy novel is *The Water of Possibility*. She has two children and learns more about being a mother every day.

SUE GOYETTE has published a book of poems, *The True Names of Birds,* which was short-listed for the Governor General's Award, the Pat Lowther Award, and the Gerald Lampert Award. Her novel, *Lures,* was published in 2002. Her next book of poetry, *Undone,* will be published in 2004. She lives on the east coast with her two teenagers.

NANCY LEE's story collection, *Dead Girls,* was short-listed for the Pearson Canada Readers' Choice Award and named Book of the Year by *Now Magazine.* She is the recipient of numerous prizes, including the prestigious Gabriel Award for Radio and a National Magazine Award.

MELANIE LITTLE's writing has appeared in *The Malahat Review, subTerrain, Prairie Fire,* and *Event,* and in the anthologies *Scribners Best of the Fiction Workshops, Outskirts,* and *Nerves Out Loud.* Her first book, the story collection *Confidence,* was published in 2003.

SUSAN MUSGRAVE has been nominated, and has received awards, in five different categories of writing. In her spare time she drives a car covered with thousands of glued-on toys. She edited *Nerves Out Loud: Critical Moments in the Lives of Seven Teen Girls* and *You Be Me: Friendship in the Lives of Teen Girls.*

TAIEN NG-CHAN is the editor of *ribsauce: a cd/anthology of words by women* and reviews editor at *Matrix Magazine.* Her poetry and fiction have been published in a number of anthologies and journals, and she has written drama for the stage and for radio. She lives in Montreal.

GAYLA REID's fiction often deals with her childhood in Australia. She contributed to *You Be Me,* the previous anthology in this series. Her most recent work of adult fiction is a collection of linked short stories entitled *Closer Apart.*

PRISCILA UPPAL has published three collections of poetry as well as the novel *The Divine Economy of Salvation.* She is a Professor of Humanities at York University, where she teaches creative writing.

Going Crazy, Wanna Come?

Susan Musgrave

"I don't advocate drugs, alcohol, violence or insanity—but they've always worked for me."

I began my convocation speech to a high school graduating class several years ago by quoting the journalist Hunter S. Thompson. I said insanity was what had *kept* me sane throughout high school because, among other things, my teeth weren't straight enough for me to be a cheerleader. Most of the graduates I was addressing came from goal-oriented upper-middle-class families. "Forget about goals," I told them. "Sigmund Freud said death is the goal of all life. Sooner or later you'll all reach your goal, so try to live a little in the meantime." The teachers told me afterwards it was the first speech they'd ever seen their students listen to.

The next day twenty outraged parents phoned the principal to complain. I was pleased that, almost thirty years after I had dropped out of high school, I still had the ability to annoy so many parents. I figured I must be doing *something* right.

I've never been the kind of writer who believes she can change the world, but I've always believed it's a writer's job to shake things up, to disturb the status quo. My teachers used to tell me I had the wrong attitude. As far as I'm concerned, it's the only kind of attitude to have. I'm happy to say this particular principal supported me, which is more than my own high school principal had done. When I ended up in his office for necking with my boyfriend instead of paying attention in Biology, "the Monk" (as we called him because of the hair growing out of his ears) told me that if I continued on this downward spiral of kissing boys, writing poetry, and skipping classes, I would most likely end up as a prostitute. But I already knew the world's oldest profession wasn't for me. I didn't want a job where you had to work with other people.

I don't think there is one moment when you realize, This is it, this is who I am, what has just happened to me is going to change my life forever. Instead there are a series of life-altering moments, beginning when you are born and ending when you die, and a great many of these seem to occur in your teenage years.

The Skinny One

Karen Rivers

I was always the skinny one. It is my role in this family. I have two sisters. Diane is the oldest one, far enough away in age to be separate, other. She is at university, in a different world. Sonja is the middle one, eighteen months older than me, one grade ahead. She is direct and immediate competition. Here are her roles: *the pretty one, the popular one, the one who gets in trouble.* She is also the fat one. But there is some blurring of that line now, because Sonja is beginning to fade away. She has been on a diet since the seventh grade, but suddenly it is working. She eats rice cakes layered over with peanut butter so thin it is translucent and then she works it off in the gym.

She is the pretty one. But I am the smart one. I am the good one. *I am the skinny one.* If she takes skinny then all I am left with is smart and good, and that is not enough. It smacks too much of nerd, of goody-goody.

I don't put anything on *my* rice cakes at all. Peanut

butter is, after all, just flavored fat and oil. I don't need it. I take a rice cake to school for lunch and eat it in front of my locker—fast, before anyone can see me and comment—leaving small pebbly crumbs on the waxed floor. I go to the cafeteria with my friends. *I've already eaten,* I tell them. *I was starving and I couldn't wait.* I buy my diet soda and sip it slowly. I watch them eat. One girl eats an apple fritter every day. She isn't skinny. *Who does she think she is?* An apple fritter! A thousand calories of fat and sugar. I hate her for eating it. I want one so badly my chest aches and my head gets light. The empty sweetness of the diet soda turns over and over in my stomach. I push my chair back so quickly it falls over. I say, *I have to go to the library. I forgot.* I hurry away, head down, heart pounding, my mouth sore from craving so strongly what I am not allowed to have.

Not *allowed.* Says who? Me. I won't allow it.

The Popularity Plan

Aislinn Hunter

Grade 9

How it looked to everyone else

A crowd of girls, in the requisite kilts and blouses, are walking from one side of our high school campus to the other. They move in that golden kind of slow motion reserved for girl-gets-guy teen movies: kilts swish, hair is flipped casually over shoulders, textbooks are held in the crooks of their arms. When they reach the street, cars stop to let them pass. One of the girls, Kate, lowers her chin and winks at the male driver who's waving her across. She's like something out of a skin-care commercial—big smile, white teeth, perfect complexion, blonde highlights in light-brown hair. Over by the parking lot a few grade twelve basketball all-stars are watching the girls. They're leaning against a sporty green Alfa Romeo, and when they see the girls looking, they wave. Debbie, a girl with dark hair in long braids, rolls her eyes, waves back. Then the girls carry on. All eight of them, the sun shining down on them as they enter the doors of St. Anne's Secondary, heading in for class.

How it looked to me

Kate is bulldozing her way across campus with all of us in tow. I'm trying to keep up. It's spring, and the gang has dressed for it—Esprit blouses tucked into kilts, a short-sleeved Guess button-down on Caroline, Debbie in a crew-neck Ralph Lauren. The kilt and cardigan are part of the mandatory uniform, but we can wear whatever kind of white top we want. I hold my books in front of me like a shield. Under my cardigan I'm wearing a big Hanes T-shirt I took out of my brother's closet. It hangs down over the pleats of my kilt, making me look as large as a semi. I'm obviously "the fat one." And my hair is too short to flip. Walking en masse, we head across the road. Kate is talking about next week's party at Caroline and Christy's house. Who to invite, who to avoid. I listen in.

Over by the parking lot, some of the grade twelve guys wave in our direction. They're always hanging around our lockers and inviting us to after-game parties, even though we're only in grade nine. Next year all the girls I'm walking with will go to the prom, although we'll still be two years away from being seniors. Not me, though. I won't get asked. That kind of thing is a given.

Good in a Group

Anne Fleming

Twelve

In the dining room, filling out the forms that will match me up with a kid from Quebec for my pending *visite interprovinciale,* my mother and I have a big fight. You have to put a tick next to "outgoing" or "reserved." Mom insists I am reserved. I say I'm outgoing. In fact, both are true. I'm socially outgoing and emotionally reserved, though I don't have the wherewithal at age twelve to make that distinction. Mom wins the fight, as she usually does. I end up with a painfully shy and awkward girl with whom I have nothing in common. Describing her later to friends, I slap a thumb-and-forefinger L to my fore-head and say "Loser!" But that's not the point here.

The point here is about being socially outgoing but emotionally reserved. This means a number of things for my friendships: 1) They tend to be less about the exchange of intimacies than the exchange of jokes; 2) They start in the public sphere—in class, in the halls, at band rehearsal, in the showers after swim practice, on the way to track meets, on ski team road trips—and stay there unless the other person initiates. Calling people up and asking them to do things makes me feel like a porcupine with its belly exposed. Bad enough to reveal you like someone, but to reveal you presume they might like you too? Aaaaaah. Too vulnerable, too vulnerable; 3) I am good in a group.

I love groups. Yeah, they can be exclusionary and dangerous, cliquey and inwardly conformist and yada yada, but even so they can be fabulous. And then there are the moments of true groupness, those rare but exquisite times when it feels everyone is equal and respected and liked, when it's clear you're all wonderful, inventive, funny people and that you're in this together, whatever *this* is.

Acting Lessons

Cathy Stonehouse

Lately, what I've been scared of is personal questions. The magazines are full of them. Is your skin dry, oily, or a combination? Are you an introvert or an extrovert? I study the articles at home and under my desk at school. I also watch TV and observe my classmates closely. All I want is to blend in and not be noticed. Yet as soon as I've figured out what's expected, what it is I'm supposed to know about myself, the rules change.

Take friends, for instance. Until about a year ago, everyone at school had a best friend. Now suddenly everyone's in groups. What's more, these groups talk only about boyfriends. If you don't have one, you are expected to want one, and to drop the names of all the boys you've kissed in the meantime. Then at least everyone knows you're normal and not stuck-up, frigid, or a lesbian. I'm not really sure what I am, nor do I feel any urgency to find out. The thought of having sex fills me with dread, and allowing some acne-faced fifteen-year-old to stick his hand up my skirt at the church hall disco is not exactly my idea of romance. But I wouldn't say no to friendship; in fact, I'm desperate for it.